News and Democratic
Citizens in the Mobile Era

Oxford Studies in Digital Politics

Series Editor: Andrew Chadwick, Professor of Political Communication in the Centre for Research in Communication and Culture and the Department of Social Sciences, Loughborough University

News and Democratic Citizens in the Mobile Era

JOHANNA DUNAWAY AND KATHLEEN SEARLES

OXFORD
UNIVERSITY PRESS

Oxford University Press is a department of the University of Oxford. It furthers
the University's objective of excellence in research, scholarship, and education
by publishing worldwide. Oxford is a registered trade mark of Oxford University
Press in the UK and certain other countries.

Published in the United States of America by Oxford University Press
198 Madison Avenue, New York, NY 10016, United States of America.

Library of Congress Cataloging-in-Publication Data
Names: Dunaway, Johanna, author. | Searles, Kathleen, author.
Title: News and Democratic Citizens in the Mobile Era /
Johanna Dunaway, Kathleen Searles.
Description: New York, NY : Oxford University Press, [2023] |
Series: Oxford studies digital politics series |
Includes bibliographical references and index.
Identifiers: LCCN 2022026958 (print) | LCCN 2022026959 (ebook) |
ISBN 9780190922498 (paperback) | ISBN 9780190922504 (hardback) |
ISBN 9780190923808 (epub)
Subjects: LCSH: News audiences. | Smartphones—Psychological aspects. |
Smartphones—Social aspects. | Journalism—Technological innovations. |
Communication and technology—Psychological aspects. | Digital divide. | Attention.
Classification: LCC PN4784.N48 D86 2023 (print) | LCC PN4784.N48 (ebook) |
DDC 302.23—dc23/eng/20220811
LC record available at https://lccn.loc.gov/2022026958
LC ebook record available at https://lccn.loc.gov/2022026959

DOI: 10.1093/oso/9780190922504.001.0001

9 8 7 6 5 4 3 2 1

Paperback printed by Lakeside Book Company, United States of America
Hardback printed by Bridgeport National Bindery, Inc., United States of America

To Frank Feigert, a career-long mentor, in memory of Manny Patel, a cherished best friend, and in memory of Martin Johnson, who was both.
—Johanna Dunaway

To Winfield and his namesake, my wholemakers. And in memory of Martin Johnson, who always made reading on a smartphone look good. I miss you, friend.
—Kathleen Searles

Contents

Acknowledgments

Key parts of this project would not be possible without the contributions of Mingxiao Sui, Newly Paul, and Stuart Soroka. Mingxiao and Newly worked with us as graduate research assistants at Louisiana State University when we designed and conducted the eye-tracking lab studies presented in Chapters 5 and 7. They helped program and execute the studies conducted at the Media Effects Lab at LSU. They also assisted with the extraction, cleaning, and analysis of the data presented in our related article on mobile news attention published in the *Journal of Computer-Mediated Communication*. Their contributions were invaluable. We are grateful for their help, hard work, and collaborative spirit. Stuart was not only a key collaborator on the psychophysiological study presented in Chapter 6, he was a sounding board and encouraging reader and critic from the very earliest stages of the idea. The experiment we present in Chapter 7 was also modeled after those from Stuart's earlier work. We appreciate his willingness (and that of his collaborators) to share elements of their designs and for the insights we draw from their original work. We especially wish to thank Patrick Fournier and Lilach Nir, who helped develop some of the physiological protocols and sentiment coding we used in our work. We also appreciate help from several research assistants at the University of Michigan, including Dominic Valentino, Jewel Drigo, and Colvin Larance.

We are also thankful for numerous insightful comments from faculty and fellows at the Joan Shorenstein Center for Media, Politics, and Public Policy in 2015. Matt Baum, Joanna Jolly, Marion Just, Dan Kennedy, Tom Patterson, Victor Pickard, and Marilyn Thompsen were especially helpful as regular attendees of our regular Monday project development meetings. Similarly, we are indebted to Vin Arceneaux (as host) and the participants at the 2016 Experimental Approaches to Studying Democratic Politics Conference at Princeton University, participants at the 2016 Post Election Research Conference hosted by the Wesleyan Media Project, participants at the 2017 conference on

Visions in Methodology at Stony Brook University, participants at the 2017 St. Louis Area Methods Meeting, and participants at the annual Omnibus Methods Group Meetings. At these venues we received tremendously valuable feedback and encouragement.

We are also grateful to the following departments and universities for hosting talks about this project, including the Departments of Political Science and Communication at Temple University, the Department of Political Science at the University of Alabama, the Valencia School of Communication and the Department of Political Science at the University of Houston, the University of Amsterdam Digital Communication Lab, the Department of Political Science at Elon University, the Department of Communication Studies at the University of Kansas, the Department of Political Science at Stony Brook University, the Department of Political Science at Skidmore University, the Department of Political Science at Purdue University, the Department of Communication Studies at University of Michigan, the Department of Political Science at South Alabama University, FLACSO University, the Department of Political Science at the University of Kentucky, and the Department of Political Science at the University of Massachusetts, Lowell. We also thank Talia Stroud and the attendees of the Political Communication Lecture Series in the Department of Communication Studies at the University of Texas at Austin. Talia was kind enough to coordinate the talk at which she and her colleagues and students provided extremely valuable feedback. At Texas A&M, we thank the Department of Communication, the Department of Psychology, and the Department of Political Science for invitations to give talks and for excellent comments and questions.

We are particularly grateful to Kirby Goidel and Paul Kellstedt. In addition to inviting us to give a talk at the Department of Communication, Kirby read and provided feedback on early drafts of *several* chapters. He also served as a regular encourager and sounding board. Paul invited us to present to the Political Institutions and Behavior Speaker Series in the Department of Political Science, where we received especially insightful comments from friends and colleagues at A&M.

We are also indebted to Hart Blanton, Nour Zeid, Samantha Ashbell, Madelyn Phillips, and the other members of the Texas A&M Department of Communication's MIRI (Media Effects Research Internship) group, who were kind enough to read drafts and endure several presentations in which we workshopped issues with which we were wrestling. Kevin Barge, Hart Blanton, and the wonderful staff in the Department of Communication at A&M helped us secure space, equipment, and research assistants for the psychophysiological experiments hosted at Texas A&M. We also owe a debt of gratitude to the LSU Manship School of Mass Communication, through which Katie has the Darlene and Thomas O Ryder Professorship, funding which made much of this work possible. Also, the Media Effects Lab at LSU, under the direction of Director Meghan Sanders, was essential to the success of this project.

Several student research assistants at Texas A&M contributed to this project and deserve our sincere gratitude. Jordan Dickerson and Jarrod Romine assisted with running the psychophysiological experiments at A&M. Nour Zeid and Brook Reichardt provided invaluable assistance with chapter editing; for this we also thank Joshua DiCaglio from the Department of English at Texas A&M, for his program offering faculty student editing assistance from students in his class. We thank Leon "Cockeye" Kockaya for his painstaking assistance with formatting and references as we finalized the documents for submission to OUP. Justin Weng, Patrick Rose, Jacob Harvey, Levi Bankston, and other members of the LSU Political Attitudes and Campaigns Research Group also assisted with various research tasks.

Several of our friends and colleagues endured more than one presentation from this project. To these friends we owe both our apologies and thanks; all offered valuable suggestions and encouragement each time: Vin Arceneaux, Hart Blanton, Lindita Camaj, Scott Campbell, Joshua Darr, Jessica Feezell, Kirby Goidel, Jennifer Jerit, Martin Johnson, Yanna Krupnikov, Ashley Muddiman, David Nickerson, Jaime Settle, Stuart Soroka, Talia Stroud, and Chris Wlezien. Several other friends and colleagues heard so much about it over the years they might as well have attended numerous talks, including Bert Bakker, Emily Beaulieu, Nadia Brown, Amber Boydstun, Scott Cook, Bill and Laurie Clark, Scott Clifford, Belinda and Dan Davis, Claes de Vreese, Tasha Dubriwny, Erika Franklin Fowler, Jim Garand, Beth Goidel, Jess Havens, Matthew Hayes, Mirya Holman, Eric Juenke, Jennifer Jerit, David Karpf, Deb Kellstedt, Samara Klar, Daniel Kreiss, Regina Lawrence, Yph Lelkes, Christine Lipsmeyer, Shannon McGregor, Diana Z. O'Brien, Jakob Ohme, Valentina Parma, Erik Peterson, Kristan Poirot, Markus Prior, Travis Ridout, Maya Sen, Paru Shah, Michael Wagner, Cara Wallis, Brian Weeks, Guy Whitten, Matt Woods, and Dannagal Young. We sincerely appreciate their patience, comments, and encouragement.

This project also benefited from helpful comments and insights provided by several editors and anonymous reviewers. We are grateful to the various reviewers who commented on our work along the way, and we especially appreciate those provided by the referees enlisted to review the project for OUP. Relatedly, we would be remiss if we failed to acknowledge the expertise, assistance, and encouragement provided by the editors at OUP—we are enormously grateful to Angela Chnapko, our Acquisitions Editor, and Andrew Chadwick, Series Editor for Oxford Studies in Digital Politics.

Finally, we wish to acknowledge the help and encouragement of our families and friends from outside our professional circles. For Johanna, those include

Pace Pipes, Suzanne Jones, Jennalee Jones, Jessica Ingram, Mauricio Escobar, Mike Choate, Toby Pipes, Dave Lane, Tim and Misty Locke, Heather Lujan, Jenny Simons, Marissa Stabler, Katy Wagner, Sherry and Jeff Woodahl, Taylor Young, and the women in wine club.

Katie would like to thank Winnie and John, the two people that make it all worthwhile, and Mark and Beth, the two people that made it all possible.

1

Gaining Access and Losing Information

Mobile phones are ubiquitous. Approximately eighty percent of U.S. adults say they use their smartphones to access news sometimes or often (Walker 2019), and most of the popular news websites now attract more mobile visitors than desktop visitors (Lu and Holcomb 2016). The majority of Americans don't just own smartphones; they increasingly rely on mobile devices for internet access. Many are abandoning home high-speed broadband service entirely, opting to depend on their smartphones instead (Pew 2021). The mobile era is here, and its embrace by politicians, campaigns, the news industry, and the public has far-reaching implications. In this book, we examine the consequences of mobile proliferation for the ability of democratic citizens to get the information they need.

The wide and growing reach of mobile internet access creates the potential to erase lingering digital divides (Grantham and Tsekouras 2004; Boyera 2007). Whether mobile communication technologies realize this potential remains in dispute (see Mossberger et al. 2012; Mossberger et al. 2013; Pearce and Rice 2013; Napoli and Obar 2014; Donner 2015). There is little doubt that mobile communication technology is expanding the scope of physical access to news and political information. And yet, there are two seemingly conflicting accounts for what this means.

The first account lauds the expansion of mobile access because it affords more people access to the internet. It depicts mobile devices as a stopgap for those without affordable access to quality high-speed internet, which varies across geographic, socioeconomic, and political boundaries (Weidmann et al. 2016). Extant research points to gains in mobile use by young people, those with lower incomes, in rural settings, and in racial and ethnic minority groups (Smith 2010; Zickuhr and Smith 2012; Mossberger et al. 2013).

The second account suggests mobile devices are not the great leveler they are purported to be. Quality high speed internet access facilitates seeking news

News and Democratic Citizens in the Mobile Era. Johanna Dunaway and Kathleen Searles, Oxford University Press. © Oxford University Press 2023. DOI: 10.1093/oso/9780190922504.003.0001

online and gains in political knowledge (Mossberger et al. 2012b; Lelkes 2016). However, evidence suggests that mobile only access is not a sufficient replacement (Mossberger et al. 2013; Pearce and Rice 2013; Napoli and Obar 2014). Information seeking and processing are more difficult on mobile devices relative to computers with high-speed internet connections; as a result, mobile users engage in fewer "capital enhancing" activities (Pearce and Rice 2013). Searching for information (Chae and Kim 2004) and learning from mobile devices is also challenging (Maniar et al. 2008). Information is hard to find and more difficult to recall on mobile devices. Cord-cutting respondents from Pew's internet project report that abandoning high speed wireless access makes keeping up with the news much more difficult (Dunaway 2016). According to this account, those dependent on mobile devices for internet access are part of an "emergent internet underclass" (Napoli and Obar 2014) or "second class digital citizens" (Mossberger et al. 2013).

What accounts for these two differing explanations of the impact of mobile devices? We argue research on mobile technology and democracy has yet to seriously consider the different ways in which mobile devices structure access to information. We address this issue by reviving an important distinction between *physical* and *cognitive* access (Grabe et al. 2000a) and applying it to the case of mobile news. Physical access to information refers to the extent to which technological infrastructure (the adequacy of hardware, software, and connections), market offerings, and costs associated with obtaining and using communication technologies afford the opportunity to encounter information (Dimaggio and Hargittai 2001). Cognitive access refers to the ease with which information is processed, once exposure occurs (Grabe et al. 2000a). Building on this early work in media effects, we consider the possibility that even as mobile technology increases the opportunity for exposure (Mossberger et al. 2013) it does so alongside increased constraints on information processing (Detenber and Reeves 1996; Grabe et al. 2000a; Dunaway et al. 2018). Putting it succinctly: even if it is the case that mobile technology facilitates widespread *physical* access to information, the constraints it imposes on *cognitive* access limits information processing.

This distinction between physical and cognitive access is important because it helps us accomplish two central objectives. First, it helps us reconcile contrasting descriptions of mobile effects by demonstrating that mobile can expand access to political information in some ways (Donner and Walton 2013), while limiting it in others (Grabe et al. 2000a). Doing so advances the literature on mobile communication technology. By situating studies of mobile effects in the context of media effects, a focus on physical and cognitive access also helps us attain our second, broader, objective, which is to demonstrate the need for a new approach to studying technological change and media effects, one capable of accommodating changes to communication infrastructures and the proliferation of platforms and devices.

In this book, we explore media effects in the context of today's high-choice and multi-platform media environment. In recent years, the media environment has experienced constant flux, populated by a dizzying array of platforms available on a growing number of devices of varying sizes and capabilities. Our primary interest is in how media consumption on these different devices and platforms affects the acquisition of political information. We investigate this question against the backdrop of the history of media effects research, with particular interest in an ongoing debate about the return of minimal effects (Bennet and Iyengar 2008), and amidst claims about the capability of mobile devices to eradicate lingering digital divides. We argue that today's array of platforms and devices are capable of structuring media messages in ways that affect their post-exposure processing. These effects can occur due to differences in message presentation borne from the specific features of devices like mobile phones as well as social media platforms like Facebook. Specifically, information communication technologies have important effects on the cognitive accessibility of media messages, with consequences for how people attend to these messages and ultimately, what they can learn from them.

As we shall see, despite advances in research on how technological advancements affect media choice and selectivity (Prior 2005; Ohme et al. 2016; Stroud 2008, 2011), existing theories of media and democracy have not evolved to provide an integrated framework to explain how communication technologies affect information delivery in ways that shape cognitive access, or, the ease with which information is attended to and processed. *This gap limits our ability to fully understand how fundamental changes in communication technology alter what we currently know about media effects.*

The theoretical contribution of this book is to address this gap. We draw on literature across several fields to develop a more complete theoretical framework that explains how communication technology structures both physical and cognitive access to information, and specifically, the ways in which mobile communication technologies shape news consumption and effects. Although we apply the framework to mobile media consumption in this book, it can be usefully applied to other cases as demonstrated by examples in later chapters.

Motivating this framework is the argument that technology affects the opportunity for exposure to information—including the motivation to avoid or choose it—and once exposed, how individuals process content. The latter part of this argument is an important revision to the opportunity-motivation-ability (OMA) framework which explained political learning from media as a function of a person's opportunity for exposure, motivation for consuming content, and their ability to do so (Delli Carpini and Keeter 1996; Prior 2007). Importantly,

OMA treats ability as a fixed individual-level trait while we understand individuals' ability to process information as constrained by contextual and situational considerations.[1] Our framework emphasizes that communication technologies affect the media environment with implications for media preferences and consumption behaviors which operate pre-exposure, through market level effects on media choice as outlined above. But they also operate through message content and structure, the effects of which occur post-exposure.

We pose a framework based on physical and cognitive access (PCA), which we use to identify and explain important mobile effects in today's media environment, and which provides a means to develop and test expectations for the effects of changing communication technology. The PCA framework helps us advance theory by elucidating the relative neglect of attention and post-exposure processes generally in post-broadcast media effects research. After shifting our focus to address this gap, we develop a model to explain technological effects on post-exposure processing (PEP). Before we discuss the PCA and PEP in detail, we briefly situate our broader arguments in existing research.

News and Mobile Technology

With each major shift in communication technology, observers have worried over how it affects what the public knows, an important consideration given an informed citizenry is a requisite for functioning democracy. News and political information seeking are important for civic life (Campbell and Kwak 2010; Shah et al. 2005). For generations, traditional news media informed the public and enriched democratic citizenship (Graber and Dunaway 2018). Recent advances in communication technology opened additional avenues through which those interested in news and information can be more engaged in civic life (Shah et al. 2005). Naturally, scholars and practitioners are interested in the democratic and economic consequences of changes in the information technology landscape. A robust literature on the political and civic implications of internet proliferation, for example, suggests higher levels of political engagement among those using the internet for news, exchanging information, and exploring interests (Kwak et al. 2004; Shah et al. 2005). It is clear from this work that the next important frontier of technological change with democratic consequences is mobile; researchers continue to speculate about the effects of mobile devices on a host of political and social outcomes, both positive and negative.

A lot of early evidence about mobile technology suggests room for optimism. Research on mobile technology in developing settings (Brown, Campbell, and Ling 2011; Donner and Walton 2013; Gitau, Marsden, and Donner 2010), for example, finds several avenues through which mobile devices can improve digital inclusion and learning, economic development, and quality of life. Statistics on smartphone proliferation and wireless mobile access reveal steep gains in access among those historically disadvantaged by digital divides, prompting many to credit mobile as an important vehicle for inclusion and digital citizenship (Grantham and Tsekouras 2004; Boyera 2007). There seems to be little doubt that mobile communication technology is expanding physical access to information, but we are skeptical about mobile's potential to eradicate lingering digital divides. We are particularly skeptical about the likelihood mobile proliferation will play a democratic role in producing a more informed citizenry.

The problem with the idea that mobile technology, through sheer audience reach, will increase rates of political knowledge and participation is that it belies everything we know about the high-choice media environment (Prior 2007). Mobile is a high-choice platform, after all, which means that by providing constant access to innumerable sources of both news and entertainment, its impact as a provider of political information will be muted by the simple fact that most of the public has a preference for entertainment over news (Prior 2007; Arceneaux and Johnson 2013). Even if people do choose to consume news on mobile devices, this perspective fails to appreciate how mobile devices structure and present information differently than television sets, radios, or personal computers. Additionally, mobile devices structure information in ways that make information harder to process and to seek out in the first place (Napoli and Obar 2014).

And still, increased reach does not guarantee exposure, nor does exposure equate to attention. Mounting evidence, including the results presented in this book, suggests attention is more limited on mobile devices, offsetting some gains in physical access to news and political information (Napoli and Obar 2014).

This trade-off—between technologically-driven effects on physical access to information and cognitive access to information—is something media effects research has documented with previous iterations of technological change. Extant research shows how television news broadened knowledge for those previously unexposed but weakened it for those who ultimately substituted television news for newspapers. Although previously untapped news audiences were reached with television; the depth of exposure was less than that for traditional newspaper audiences (Prior 2007). Movement from the partisan press to penny presses tells a similar story (Starr 2004). The literature on changing communication technologies and media effects is clear—the way communication technologies affect physical access to information is only part of the story—how the news is presented and how people process it matters (Grabe et al. 2000a).

Placing mobile in the context of research on media effects helps us understand the impact of mobile technology on the media's ability to influence and underscores the need to change the way we study media effects more generally.

We situate our work in the history of media effects research next, before pre-viewing our approach. This review of the literature provides insights integral to our call for integrating changes in communication technology and media effects.

Technological Change and Media Effects

Media effects research examines media impact on the mass public. It is partic-ularly important for democracies, as democratic theory requires the public be informed of the doings of their elected officials, and the media is still the primary way the public learns of politics. It also addresses questions affecting the balance of power between elites and the mass public with potentially profound results for media influence on public opinion. In this context, changes in communica-tion technology matter for the public because they affect the costs of seeking political information. This is one reason why paradigm shifts in effects research have historically coincided with major changes in communication technology. Indeed, a century's worth of scholarship on media effects began with the arrival of radio and television, motivated by concerns over the persuasive influence of propaganda following World War II (Iyengar 2017; Jamieson 2017).

Despite the rich history of media effects studies, the challenge of demonstrat-ing the impact of mass media has proved daunting for researchers. As a result, decades of research reveal a pattern of dramatic pendulum swings about the extent to which media can influence opinions, attitudes, and behaviors. The theoretical, conceptual, and methodological challenges underlying this instabil-ity have varied over time, but a few notable obstacles have resurfaced at critical junctures. These obstacles can be characterized in three ways: One is to conflate *access* to information with *exposure* to information. A second is to conflate *expo-sure* to information with *attention* to information. A third is a disproportionate focus on how media affects persuasion and attitude change relative to learning, reinforcement, and other important effects. Over time, problems of measure-ment and method have been both a cause and consequence of these tendencies. Our call for a new approach is informed by these persistent challenges.

MEDIA EFFECTS IN THE BROADCAST ERA

Media effects research was premised on a conflation between access and expo-sure to information, one that misinformed the era of direct and powerful media effects. Responding to normative concerns about government propaganda, and dramatic changes to the form and dissemination of media messages, researchers anticipated direct and powerful media influence over public opinion (Iyengar and Kinder 1987). Assuming audiences were eager and passive recipients of information, and that access to media messages was equivalent to exposure, they believed the reach and format of broadcast media would make its messages too powerful to resist (Bineham 1988). "Magic Bullet" and "Hypodermic Needle" theories were developed to explain expectations for direct and powerful effects (Iyengar 2017; Jamieson 2017).

Despite the early concerns about an all-powerful broadcast media and mass persuasion, by the middle of the twentieth century, evidence casted doubt on this view. Studies showed that audiences are capable of making choices about what media to consume, according to their individual preferences and tastes (Lazarsfeld, Berelson, and Gaudet 1948, 151; Jamieson 2017; Iyengar 2017). Focusing on what we refer to as *pre-exposure processes*—what occurs before individuals are exposed to media messages such as selectivity and choice—these studies, later characterized as part of the minimal effects paradigm, highlighted the difference between access and exposure to information. They showed that just because a new media technology expands access to information, selective exposure—the act of deliberately choosing specific media messages to attend to or ignore—means that access does not necessarily translate to exposure (Jamieson 2017; Iyengar 2017). Although now familiar, the concept of selective exposure was a radical departure from the assumptions of uniform exposure that characterized early work on media effects (Smith, Fabrigar, and Norris 2008). During this period, selective exposure was cited as one of the key explanations for why media effects were minimal (Jamieson 2017; Iyengar 2017).

Minimal effects studies were successful in debunking "hypodermic needle" theories, but they also produced an overcorrection. In response to a lack of demonstrable persuasive effects, media effects research shifted dramatically from predictions of massive and direct effects to the belief that media were capable of affecting the mass public only minimally. This shift occurred even as television proliferated rapidly into American households. Prolonged subscription to the minimal effects view was attributable to four things: a single-minded focus on persuasion, conflation between access and exposure, conflation between exposure and attention, and limited methodological approaches. The focus on persuasion that characterized early effects research was problematic primarily for its role in propping up the minimal effects paradigm. The pursuit of attitude change and the failure to find evidence for it supported the belief that media were rarely influential, delaying the discovery of other media effects until the 1970s (Jamieson 2017; Iyengar 2017).

The era of minimal effects was also prolonged by the continuing tendency to conflate access and exposure to political information. While in pursuit of persuasive effects, researchers (studying campaign advertisements in particular) largely failed to account for message-level characteristics constraining the likelihood of people's exposure. A reliance on survey instruments lead to the erroneous attribution of null effects to campaigns' inability persuade, when it was just as likely a product of low exposure (Zaller 1992, 1996).

A more pressing issue was the conflation between exposure and attention. Despite previous work showing that attention follows exposure, is not automatic, and is conditional on individual-level motivations and abilities (McGuire 1968), minimal effects studies consistently blurred the lines between exposure and attention. In doing so, this work assumed that once people were exposed to a message, they processed it. Null findings were considered evidence of an absence of persuasion, when they likely reflected message inattention (Zaller 1996). It was not until Zaller (1992), motivated by McGuire's (1968) insights, reaffirmed the important distinction between exposure and attention that researchers began to recognize the need to account for individual-level and contextual characteristics when studying persuasion.

Other researchers argued that audio visual media could have powerful influence despite early failures to demonstrate direct and powerful media effects (e.g., Iyengar and Kinder 1987). They focused on indirect effects resulting from attributes of messages, such as production choices, and the news-making process, such as story selection.

Iyengar and Kinder (1987) also helped demonstrate that limits in common methodological approaches were to blame for some of the theoretical and conceptual challenges that persisted during this period. Like Zaller (1996), Iyengar and Kinder (1987) attributed persistent findings of minimal effects to the difficulty of accurately capturing individual-level news exposure. The inability to capture people's news diets meant that even accounting for political interest, researchers could never actually be sure about which media messages people were exposed to or the extent to which they paid attention once exposed. Iyengar and Kinder (1987) argued for the need to introduce experiments to the study of media effects. With control over stimuli and randomization, experiments gave researchers the ability to isolate the causal effects of media messages while randomization mitigates concerns regarding differences between the treatment groups. The control afforded by experiments also enables researchers to ensure treatment delivery and collect data on attention, ensuring no conflation between exposure and attention. Moreover, lab subjects typically abide by the instructions researchers give them, and manipulation checks offer a means by which to ensure participant compliance. By using these methods to demonstrate other important media effects besides persuasion, Iyengar and Kinder (1987) encouraged scholars to look beyond persuasion for evidence of media effects and helped usher in widespread use of experimental methods in studies of media effects. These works were among a key few that were fundamental to overcoming several theoretical and methodological challenges, contributing to a consensus that media are capable of powerful but limited effects.

Indeed, the theoretical advances made during this period are owed, at least in part, to scholars' recognition of problems stemming from the conflation of exposure and attention in the study of media effects. Zaller (1992) did so by again elevating McGuire's insight that persuasion requires both receipt and acceptance of messages, both of which require attention. He also highlighted the role that motivation plays in exposure to political information, providing a reminder that access is not equivalent to exposure. Zaller theorized that minimal effects findings were a product of low exposure, low attention, or resistance based on predispositions rather than the inability of mass media to persuade. People with high levels of interest in politics might be high on the exposure dimension, but low on the acceptance dimension due to firmly held predispositions. Alternatively, those low in interest are prone to acceptance but are rarely exposed to political information as they are unmotivated to seek it out (McGuire 1968; Zaller 1992; Jamieson 2017; Iyengar 2017). By identifying the limited conditions under which persuasion occurs, Zaller (1992) reasserted the crucial distinction between message exposure and message receipt and acceptance. With these advances in place, by the time the broadcast era concluded, effects research evolved to a consensus that media were capable of producing powerful, but limited media effects.

POST-BROADCAST MEDIA EFFECTS

The expansion of media choice that accompanied the arrival of cable, and later the internet, disrupted the media environment. Cable marked a gradual but massive expansion of channel offerings into households, and as high-speed internet proliferated those same options expanded to their online formats, accompanied by thousands of additional outlets for entertainment and news. Both cable and internet produced a rush of new media competitors in the marketplace, which created pressure for content providers to seek and meet unmet needs for niche programming. Shortly, more options emerged along both dimensions of news and entertainment, including partisan cable news networks (Stroud 2011; Arceneaux and Johnson 2013; Smith and Searles 2013, 2014).

These changes had significant implications for broadcast-era researchers' understanding of media effects, and once again dramatically shifted the trajectory of effects research. This is especially true with respect to scholarly treatment of the relationship between access and exposure to information and their relative focus on persuasion and political knowledge. One of the most important advances from research on the high-choice media environment and the revival of interest in selective exposure is that it has helped clarify why access to information should not be conflated with exposure to it (e.g., Prior 2007; Arceneaux and Johnson 2013). Studies of audience behavior in the high-choice media environment made clear that active audiences ignore plenty of information, despite increasing levels of access.

Unfortunately, much post-broadcast media effects research retained the disproportionate focus on persuasion and attitude change, and the tendency to conflate exposure with attention. Despite this tendency, a few notable exceptions were much more concerned about the effects of choice for political learning. Prior (2007) was among the first to anticipate the consequences of the high-choice media environment for political knowledge. His articulation of the role media environments play in political learning was instrumental in distinguishing access and exposure to information. Building on the OMA framework, Prior argued that political learning is conditional on characteristics of the media environment, which structures the opportunity for exposure to information. He described the specifics of how technology affects the media environment, explaining that it does so by determining "the media available to people at a particular place and time," and that access to some new forms of media is constrained by local technological "physical infrastructure" before access is possible. In other words, even when new media technology makes information available, the mere opportunity for access does not guarantee exposure. Even when physical access to political information is possible, exposure still depends on the perceived costs and benefits of access. Conceptually, Prior helped to distinguish the difference between physical access to information and exposure itself. This distinction is one of the important pieces that motivates our PCA framework.

The expansion of media choice and the re-emergence of partisan news in particular reasserted the importance of persuasion for effects researchers, particularly in light of audience tendencies toward selective exposure (Arceneaux and Johnson 2013). The elevation of active and heterogeneous audiences discovered during the era of minimal effects and the new high-choice media environment begged for a return to selective exposure (Stroud 2008). In contrast to their discovery during the era of minimal effects, when interest in selective exposure theories first resurged with the arrival of cable and the internet, they were not typically thought of as a means by which media effects are limited. In the face of expanding media choice, the importance of selective exposure took on new meaning, raising concerns about partisan forms of selective exposure. Many expected that when given the choice, people would choose only to hear from congenial perspectives, leading to echo chambers that would strengthen and polarize attitudes.

While not always described as persuasion outright, fears about partisan selective exposure were nonetheless about attitude change—often in the form of attitude reinforcement, partisan extremity, political polarization, or negative partisan affect (e.g., Jamieson and Cappella 2008; Stroud 2010; Levendusky 2013a, 2013b; Smith and Searles 2013, 2014). It was natural for a subfield historically concerned with the persuasive effects of media on attitude change to focus on trying to understand what this new landscape meant for partisan selective exposure and the resulting implications for political polarization.

The resurgence of selective exposure theories and the ongoing debate about media choice has meant disproportionate interest in pre-exposure processes (i.e., selectivity and choice) more generally, which again led to a tendency to conflate exposure with attention, neglecting much of what was learned of information processing. Most studies on post-exposure processing from political communication focus on the effects of congenial or non-congenial information (Stroud 2008, 2010, 2011; Levendusky 2013a, 2013b; Searles et al. 2018).[2] Hundreds of studies have been conducted on how partisan selective exposure constrains media effects, namely with an eye toward understanding effects on attitude extremity, and partisan polarization through persuasion or reinforcement (see Bennett and Iyengar 2008; Holbert et al. 2010; Prior 2013 for detailed discussions and review). Arguably, this is at the expense of research on other post-exposure effects like political learning. Relative to persuasion, post-broadcast changes to the media environment have not produced a corresponding volume of studies focused on political learning. Most exceptions (other than those referenced above) focus on how people can learn from partisan news or in a partisan news environment when partisan motivations and perceptual biases abound (e.g., Burden and Hillygus 2009; Jerit and Barabas 2012; Darr et al. 2019).

For years now, research on selective exposure and media choice has reflected the view that the most significant effect from the arrival of cable and the internet was to change the structure of market offerings (e.g., Prior 2007; Stroud 2011). And, to be fair, the changes researchers were dealing with at the time did not require an emphasis on how either cable or the internet would change exposure to content, except through choice. As of 2005, it was still unclear whether the internet would do much more than offer web-based versions of already existing print and video forms of political information, leaving the expansion of choice as the paramount source of influence on attitudes and behaviors. For some time, it seemed as if the internet would simply expand the high-choice media environment (Prior 2007).[3] But now we know that not to be true. The fact is that we have arrived full force in the multi-channel, mode, and platform era of digital, social, and mobile media. The countless platforms and devices emerging and proliferating today offer highly variable forms of message delivery and presentation. The implications for learning and persuasion—due to the changes these platforms and devices impose on the structure, display, and delivery of media messages—go beyond those spurred by market level changes to the media environment.

This is all to say that while altering the structure of market choice might be widely considered the most significant effect related to the arrival of cable and broadcast until now, more recent technological changes are emerging with new effects worthy of our attention. New devices and platforms alter the presentation of content in ways that condition attention and other aspects of cognitive access—all of which are important precursors to learning and persuasion. Cable disrupted the market, but accompanying other major post-broadcast shifts—the arrival of the internet and its wireless counterpart—is the dramatic pace of development of new platforms and devices through which citizens encounter political information. It is this setting—in which the means and opportunities for media exposure proliferate as quickly as developers can imagine them—that makes one thing abundantly clear: *current approaches to the study media effects are no longer sufficient.* If we limit our focus to pre-exposure processes and effects on persuasion and attitude change, we risk underestimating the implications of communication technologies for media effects. Given the importance of the post-broadcast media environment and the proliferation of devices and platforms: what we need now is a broad theoretical framework of technological change and media effects that can accommodate numerous iterations of technological change as well as differential effects born from the specific implications of changes in communication infrastructures, hardware and devices, and platforms alike.

The Need for a New Framework

What motivates the development of our framework is the belief that the volume and variety of rapidly developing and proliferating platforms and devices in the post-broadcast media environment (and the foreseeable future) requires a new way of thinking about communication technologies and media effects—one that gives proper attention to post-exposure information processing and the influence of technology. Just as the expansion of media choice called for a reassertion of the importance of media environments for political learning (Prior 2007), today's media environment requires a theoretical framework applicable across devices and platforms such that it can be used to understand how technologies structure information in ways that shape information processing. At the same time, any new framework must be able to reconcile these information-level effects on cognitive access with those stemming from technological effects on physical access to information, which remains crucially important to understanding media effects (Prior 2007; Stroud 2011; Arceneaux and Johnson 2013). By providing the PCA framework, and articulating the PEP theory, we hope to provide researchers with the tools they need to explain how changing communication technologies constrain attention, learning, and behavior.

Today's multi-device and platform media environment demands a framework that explains how technology impacts both physical and cognitive access to information. The application of this framework and model might be novel, but as readers will see, the argument about the importance of technological effects on information structure is more repackaged than it is new (e.g., Grabe et al. 2000a; Lang 2000). Researchers have been concerned about the way media technology structures information—and the effects on political learning and persuasion—since the earliest days of radio and television.[4]

The purpose of our framework is to illustrate technological effects that operate through pre-exposure processes on the media environment, by expanding or restricting physical access to information, and those that operate through how they structure information (i.e., changes to the display and delivery of content) and cognitive access to information.

Our primary motivation for developing this framework is the need for a model that encompasses technological effects on both pre-exposure and post-exposure processes. Thus, our model includes arguments about both stages. However, we largely focus on post-exposure processes because research on media effects and political communication has already provided a great deal of insight on how technology effects access, selectivity, and exposure. What we currently lack is a theory of how communication technologies shape content in ways that affect information processing once exposure occurs. This book addresses that gap.

Changing News Behaviors Require a Post-Exposure Focus

Changing news behaviors also motivate our advocacy for a new approach. Most current thinking about the powerful but nuanced effects of media is based on studies conducted during a time characterized by mass exposure and restricted audience choice. Although we have studied the nature of audiences since the middle of the twentieth century, the limited market for print and broadcast media meant that, for decades, consumers had few choices (Starr 2004). As choice increased alongside algorithmic filtering, the conditions for exposure to news were reduced for the persuadable and expanded for the politically interested (Bennett and Iyengar 2008). As a result, the possibility for media influence seemed substantially weakened. Indeed, the emergence of these conditions sparked a debate on whether we have entered a new era of minimal effects (Bennett and Iyengar 2008; Holbert et al. 2010).

Anticipation for a new era of minimal effects is premature, however, and born from the fact that post-exposure media effects are currently under theorized and understudied. Post-broadcast researchers' focus on technological effects at the market level (i.e., the implications of expanding media choice) has obscured interest in post-exposure effects unrelated to persuasion and attitude change. Yet, today's media environment, characterized by accessibility and availability, has altered the way news is consumed, suggesting the need to study post-exposure attention, learning, and recall (Napoli 2011). Mobile devices, for instance, encourage "snacking," where information is consumed over several smaller sessions throughout the day (Molyneux 2017); this news "grazing" is the *new* news consumption (Forgette 2019; Ohme 2019).

These and other shifts in the way news is consumed are also affecting the way news is made and monetized. News organizations and advertisers are much more interested in exposure-based measures of recall and attitude change because they are predictive of advertising clicks and purchasing behaviors. Even as early as ten years ago, we were beginning to see a shifting conceptualization of the media audience based on "a rise of alternative approaches to audience understanding" (Napoli 2011, 149). The differences are stark enough such that once these metrics converge and become effectively monetized, it will signal the migration to a *"post-exposure audience marketplace"* (Napoli 2011, 149, *emphasis in original*).[5] Scholarly focus on exposure in earlier research reflected industry measures and the best methodological capabilities at the time, when advertising rates and the monetization of news content was based on circulation numbers and Nielsen ratings. But the recent changes in media consumption and related metrics should affect how we study its impact (Forgette 2019).

The characteristics of today's media environment mandate a new approach, specifically, that we consider technological effects beyond those affecting the market and pre-exposure processes. We must also consider how communication technologies condition the effects of media messages post-exposure, acknowledging that communication technologies can shape not just *which* messages you receive, but the *manner* in which you receive them.

Summarizing the Argument

The sections above preview our argument for the PCA framework. Figure 1.1 provides a visual representation of the framework and Chapter 2 explains it in detail. To understand how changes to communication technologies shape media effects—it is important to consider two stages of the process: pre-exposure (characteristics and conditions that influence media choice and selection) and post-exposure (what happens once exposure occurs). Another important aspect of this model is the effect of the media environment on pre-exposure processes, manifest in the choices available to consumers and delivery of content. These then shape information effects, changing the breadth and depth of people's exposure. In light of extant research showing that exposure to media messages does

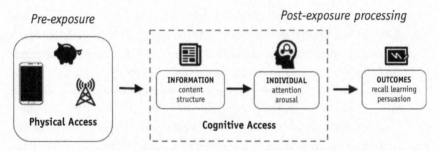

Figure 1.1 Technological effects on information access, exposure, and processing

not guarantee attention, this model underscores that—if we remain focused exclusively on how communication technologies shape media access, choice, and exposure—we cannot fully understand how information is processed once exposure occurs.

A new environment, characterized by proliferating platforms and devices for disseminating political information, calls for a more nuanced view of how communication technologies constrain information structure (the mechanics of information delivery and display) and affect media attention and political learning. Mobile devices provide an excellent test case for illustrating why researchers must differentiate between physical and cognitive access to information. Physical access to information—the technological infrastructure, the structure of market offerings, and the mediums through which information can be consumed—defines individuals' opportunity structure with regard to the information they will encounter (Prior 2007; Grabe et al. 2000a). On this front, we know much about the effect of mobile. First, it's an extension of the high-choice environment. Just as cable and the internet expanded the choice environment, mobile internet access, when coupled with a device and a subscription service, expands the choice environment by increasing the number of times and places in which one has access to information throughout the day. Second, it may expand the sphere of access beyond geographies wired for high-speed broadband. Third, it can lower the economic costs of access by circumventing the need to subscribe to high-speed home broadband plan and/or purchasing a desktop or laptop computer, which cost more than a smartphone and contract with a mobile service provider. Thus, prior work allows us to anticipate the effects of mobile for opportunity by expanding the choice environment across boundaries of space and time. For most adult smartphone users, the high-choice environment is simply always available. Opportunities are now more frequent, if not constant.

We know far less about how mobile and other newer communication technologies affect cognitive access post-exposure. While we agree with the importance of individual-level ability as defined by the OMA framework, our model provides an important revision. Ability is a critical factor in determining whether one can process, understand, and learn from news. However, communication technologies can also moderate the ability to attend news and process information even among those with even high levels of competence. They do this through their effect on the presentation of content and, in particular, how they affect the structure of information and the context. Simply put, devices display information in ways that make it easier or harder to attend to and process information regardless of ability.

Our model, which integrates our PCA framework, is a model of post-exposure processing, which posits technological effects on information structure and processing. According to the model, communication technologies exert their effects on attention and learning through their influence at the information level—on the structure of the information itself as presented by the platform or device. Thus, even after the information environment conditions the effect of *opportunity—motivation—ability* on exposure, technological effects on information structure can operate independently of, or further condition, the effects of ability and motivation by disturbing the ease with which the information is sought and processed. As we demonstrate in the next chapter, while our model yields certain expectations for the effects of mobile devices, the appeal of offering it in this general form is that the model's specific application and predictions will depend on the communication technology being investigated and its specific effects on information structure.

Our Approach

Advancing our theory is simple. Testing it is a challenge. First, it is critical to accurately measure and capture meaningful variation in attention, especially as an indicator of cognitive access. To demonstrate the relevance of technological constraints on information structure and attention for learning, we must also demonstrate that attention, as we capture it, is a precursor to information acquired from exposure to political information. Finally, we must do so in a way that separates the effects of information content from information structure. For reasons we elaborate on extensively in Chapter 4, this is difficult to achieve: the study of media politics suffers from our limited ability to accurately measure attention. Before news can be influential, it must be attended to, and attention is often elusive and fleeting, making it very difficult to reliably self-report. Difficulties with self-reported measures have been well documented in research on media exposure, which finds respondents over-estimate their news consumption (Prior 2009, 2012). As a result, more recently scholars have begun to use passive measures to capture exposure to news (Prior 2009; Ohme et al. 2016).

We adopt a multi-method strategy for dealing with challenges of measuring attention, arousal, and other markers of cognitive access thought to be precursors for learning. First, in three lab studies we use unobtrusive measures of attention and engagement based on eye tracking, heart rate variability (HRV), and skin conductance levels (SCL). Eye-tracking measures capture the visual attention stream, separating top-down cognitive processing from non-focused visual attention. Eye tracking is widely used in psychology and industry as the gold standard in measuring attention (Bode et al. 2017) and overcomes several widely-known limitations of self-report media measures (Vraga, Bode, and Troller-Renfree 2017). In the third lab study we use measures of HRV and SCL to track differences in activation and arousal in response to watching video news stories on large and small screens, corroborating our eye-tracking studies.

To overcome some of the external validity limitations of lab experiments, we employ a quasi-experimental design using a crowd-sourced labor market. Our application of this design overcomes external validity issues in two ways. First, it allows people to select their preferred device, whether computer or handheld, to participate in the study. We assume that participants reliant enough on their phones or tablets to participate in an online study are also those most likely to rely on them for media consumption.[6] Second, this design allows users to select between a political news story and an entertainment news story. Given the high rates of relative preference for entertainment content over news content, choice is important to ensure that our findings hold even in the context of entertainment content. For the final prong of our methodological strategy, we replicate our findings with real world proprietary web traffic data from Comscore.

Plan of the Book

After a full accounting of our framework, model, and expectations in Chapter 2, Chapter 3 describes the dramatic shift to mobile and offers an empirical demonstration of our PCA framework, which shows the effect of mobile technology on physical access to information. We start by examining the impact of mobile technology on audience exposure to digital news, with particular attention to differences in audiences reached across devices, and access across demographic groups.

The focus of our remaining empirical chapters is on testing our model, which examines how the content displays on mobile devices constrain cognitive access once exposure occurs. We rely primarily, but not exclusively, on psychophysiological experiments to capture cognitive access, including eye-tracking, HRV, and SCL. These psychophysiological measures may be unfamiliar to many readers, so we dedicate Chapter 4 to explaining them fully, explicating their suitability for operationalizing our central concepts.

Applying our arguments to the mobile case, in Chapter 5 we present results from the eye-tracking experiments comparing participant attention to news stories across computers, tablets, and smartphones.

What is it about the features or displays of mobile devices that affect attention? In Chapter 6, we shed light on this question by isolating the effect of screen size. Here we also demonstrate replicability and robustness by using HRV and SCL as physiological measures of interest and attention, varying the level of interestingness in the content, and by switching from text-based digital news stories to online video news content (Soroka and McAdams 2015; Daignault, Soroka, and Giasson 2013; Soroka 2014; Soroka et al. 2016).

If mobile audiences are less attentive to news stories and less aroused by their content as our theory and evidence suggests, are they still learning as much from news? This is the substantive question we address in Chapter 7, where we take up the argument that cognitive access, as measured by attention and arousal, is an important precursor to learning and recall. How much information we acquire from the news is key to assumptions about the importance of news for an informed citizenry. It is possible that information processing on mobile devices takes less time because it is more efficient. On the other hand, less time spent attending to news may mean less learning from news. Either way, it is important to understand precisely why audiences are less attentive and engaged on mobile devices. Chapter 7 presents results from a series of analyses aimed at these questions. First, we provide an extension of our eye-tracking experiments first presented in Chapter 5. Chapter 7 also presents results from Study 3, a quasi-experimental design conducted on a convenience sample, which allows people to select their preferred device, whether computer or handheld, as well as choice of their preferred content, whether political or entertainment news.

Chapter 8 reintroduces the Comscore data for some real-world tests of our key experimental findings. In Chapter 9 we review our overall findings and describe their implications for the future of news consumption and production and the possibility of an informed democratic citizenry in the mobile era. We also explain what our model suggests regarding other recent and ongoing changes in communication technology, and the usefulness of the model for explaining existing gaps and contradictions in work on media effects and changing communication technology. We argue that work on the impact of changing communication technologies needs to better differentiate between physical and cognitive access to information and to focus more on post-exposure attention. We also point to exemplars and urge the development of theories and experiments capable of explicating how technology-induced changes in the content, form, and structure of information operate in tandem with individual-level psychological traits and predispositions to produce media effects.

2

Post-Exposure Processing

A New Framework and Model

Understanding the ways in which changing communication technologies shape media effects requires attention to how changing technologies impact two processes: how people are exposed to information and how they process it once exposed. In the first part of this chapter, we propose a general framework—centered on the distinction between physical and cognitive access to information—for understanding how communication technologies affect both processes. Applying the physical and cognitive access (PCA) framework to the case of mobile, our main argument is that while mobile technology can expand opportunities for *physical* access to information, it can also affect—and sometimes limit—*cognitive* access to information. We also develop a model to explain technological effects on post-exposure processing (PEP), one that clarifies the conditions under which we should expect to see shifts in media effects in response to various changes in communication technology. In the second part of the chapter, we apply the PCA framework and PEP model to an important case: mobile communication technologies.

Our framework lays out the various means by which communication technologies can structure media effects. Some technological effects occur pre-exposure, through their influence over physical access; others occur post-exposure, through effects on cognitive access, which are dictated by an interplay between individual-level characteristics—like ability—and situational and contextual aspects affecting message content and structure—like the device or platform being used (Grabe et al. 2000a). A critical part of our argument hinges on the idea that various media forms enabled by different communication technologies shape the display and delivery of messages, altering their structure in ways that affect the individual-level ability to process information. Because different scholarly traditions have created their own terminologies to describe technological and informational characteristics, we define ours here.

News and Democratic Citizens in the Mobile Era. Johanna Dunaway and Kathleen Searles, Oxford University Press. © Oxford University Press 2023. DOI: 10.1093/oso/9780190922504.003.0002

Key Definitions

One of our principal claims is that research on media effects needs to better distinguish between physical and cognitive access to information. To be convincing on this point we need to revisit these concepts introduced in Chapter 1. When individuals or groups have *physical* access to information it means they are afforded the opportunity for exposure. Communication technologies govern physical access to information through equipment and infrastructures capable of disseminating information, such as access and choice afforded by the arrival and proliferation of broadcast technology, cable, high-speed broadband, and wireless internet connectivity. Changing communication technologies can affect whether people have physical access to any information; they can also dictate the array of information to which people have access (Prior 2007).

Alternatively, communication technologies affect *cognitive* access when they impact individuals' ability to attend and process information once exposure occurs. Motivations and abilities to attend information are highly variable and can be affected by individual, contextual, and message characteristics (Lombard et al. 1997; Hou et al. 2012). Attention can be captured through controlled or automatic processes. Controlled processes are affected by individual characteristics, such as interest in the information and the cognitive capacity for processing it. Automatic processes of attention are often triggered by characteristics of the message, such as emotionally compelling material or structural features related to things like image size or placement, and audio and video editing techniques. Cognitive access, then, is affected by communication technologies when they structure information in ways that affect processing. Most critical is their effect on the ease of processing, which is often dictated by how well messages attract attention, interest, and arouse emotion (Grabe et al. 2000a). The key insight here is the significant difference between having the opportunity for exposure to information (which has to do with physical access to information) and the motivation and ability to attend to and process that information (which has to do with cognitive access). Cognitive access, as we use it, captures the ease with which information is attended to and processed when exposure occurs. Cognitive access can be conditioned by communication technologies because they configure information in ways that affect the ease of processing. This point is where our argument is an important revision to the OMA framework. Where OMA treats A (ability) as a fixed, individual-level trait (Deli Carpini and Keeter 1996), we argue that communication technologies can situationally enhance or hamper an individual's ability to process information. As we argue in Chapter 4, it is best measured by physiological indicators of attention, emotional arousal, and cognitive effort.

We use the term "message structure" to refer to characteristics related to information provision and display, such as "display sizes, viewing angles, fidelity, resolutions, cuts, synchrony, and movements" (Hou et al. 2012, 617), and "attention-grabbing video editing and camera techniques" (Grabe et al. 2000a, 6), which are known to have important psychological effects. Others have used the term "media form" to differentiate such features from "media content" (Lombard et al. 1997; Hou et al. 2012). We opt to make this same distinction using the terms information structure and information content instead, first to avoid confusing the concept of media form with medium or media type, and, second, to ensure applicability across different sources of possible exposure to information, such as political ads, campaign messages, entertainment programs, video games, or news media.

The PCA Framework

We start by applying insights from literature across several disciplines to make two claims on which our framework and model are based: (1) communication technologies shape media effects because they dictate the boundaries of both physical and cognitive access to information, and (2) these effects operate at two stages: the pre-exposure stage and the post-exposure stage.

PRINCIPAL CLAIMS

Our first principal claim is that *communication technologies shape media effects because they dictate the boundaries of both physical and cognitive access to information.* The idea that communication technologies affect physical access to information is not new. Emerging communication technologies often offer the potential to expand the physical reach of existing media, where the potential growth is constrained only by how quickly the new technology proliferates and at what cost (Prior 2007). The arrival of broadcast radio and television, cable services, and high-speed broadband and wireless internet access all serve as good examples for how the arrival of new communication technologies changed the information environment to affect people's physical access to information, including the potential introduction of information inequalities. This tension is at the center of well-known normative concerns about digital divides, which are rooted in individual-level and place-based differences in resources (Gaziano 1983, 1997; Viswanath and Finnegan 1996; Grabe et al. 2000a; DiMaggio et al. 2004; Hargittai and Walejko 2008; van Dijk 2005; Warschauer 2003; Mossberger et al. 2013). As such, physical access to information has been of central concern to research on information inequities (Gaziano 1983, 1997; Viswanath and

Finnegan 1996) and research on the effects of expanding media choice (Stroud 2011; Prior 2005, 2007; Arceneaux and Johnson 2013).

Alternatively, the notion that communication technologies condition cognitive access to information has received intermittent attention from researchers. Building on early work in information sciences and the internet (e.g., Kling et al. 1999), Maria Grabe et al. (2000a) were among the first to apply the distinction between physical and cognitive access to the problem of how different forms of media can reduce or exacerbate information inequities. Concerned with the prevalence of knowledge gaps, they challenged the notion that television messages are universally easy to process, as largely assumed (Galloway 1977; Gantz 1978; Neuman 1976; Shingi and Mody 1976; Tichenor et al. 1970). Grabe et al. (2000a) pointed to research on information processing which indicated television may present problems for processing because of the complexity inherent to simultaneous presentations of audio-visual information streams characterized by voice, background sound, and visuals, often delivered in a distracting setting (Drew and Grimes 1987; Graber 1990; Newhagen 1998).

Primarily interested in explaining why an ostensibly high-access medium did not eliminate knowledge gaps even in a context of high-market penetration, Grabe et al. (2000) investigated whether physical access and/or cognitive access to television news differed by education level. They argued, as we do, that: (1) the motivation to attend a message, or controlled processing, varies greatly at the individual level; (2) it is governed by beliefs about the importance of information, interest in the information, and motivations for processing or avoiding the information; and (3) the automatic processes, which are not controlled by individuals, can be triggered by the characteristics of a message such as its structural features (i.e., image size and placement, compelling video edits, emotion evoking music or footage) in addition to compelling message content (Grabe et al. 2000a). Individual-level traits operate in tandem with content and information structure to shape cognitive processing. It follows that when new communication technologies change the manner in which information is delivered and displayed (i.e., through changing screen sizes or a shift from text to audio-visual), they can shape cognitive access to that information.

The second principal claim is that *these effects operate at two stages: the pre-exposure stage and the post-exposure stage.* Once we begin to make the conceptual distinction between physical and cognitive access, the reasons for several inconsistencies in the literature on communication technology become apparent. Emerging communication technologies can expand physical access to information even as they constrain cognitive access to information. Because the most recent and disruptive changes to our communication environment in recent years involved technologies' effects on the structure of market offerings (i.e., the expansion of media choice), researchers remained disproportionately focused on the consequences from those changes, all of which are a part of the pre-exposure process (e.g., Prior 2007; Stroud 2011; Arceneaux and Johnson 2013). And despite advances in research on information processing, there are fewer efforts to integrate what we know about how technology affects physical access to information pre-exposure, with everything we know about how it might affect cognitive access, post-exposure, into one theoretical framework. In short, we currently lack an explanation of technological change and media effects.

PRE-EXPOSURE EFFECTS

Some of the most profound ways in which changes to technology have an impact on media effects are by shifting the barriers of who has physical access to what information. *Communication technologies govern physical access to information through equipment and infrastructures capable of disseminating information, such as access afforded by the arrival and proliferation of broadcast technology, high-speed broadband, and wireless internet connectivity.* The arrival of broadcast radio and television into U.S. households, for example, expanded the public "news audience" because it provided the opportunity for exposure to people with a wider range of motivation and ability to attend it. For most of the public, the arrival of broadcast news was a welcome relief because it allowed viewers to be mostly passive, requiring only minimal engagement to consume (Eveland and Scheufele 2000; Kwak 1999).

Communication technology also dictates the array of information to which people have physical access by influencing the market structure of consumer choice. In the 1980s, yet more technological innovation—this time the satellite—shifted the information environment once again. As cable channels proliferated and Americans' media choices expanded, the cost of entry for media outlets was lowered, disrupting the stability of the news economy (Starr 2004). New cable news entrants, such as CNN, filled their programming with punditry and horse race coverage, expending minimal resources on serious reporting, reflecting the widely documented inverse relationship between depth in news reporting and profit-driven efforts to craft a news product with mass appeal (McManus 1994; Arnold 2004; Hamilton 2004; Starr 2004). The news audience for the major broadcast networks started to decline as these and other competitors entered the marketplace. This expansion of consumer choice had important consequences. The arrival and proliferation of high-speed internet only further expanded physical access to more sources of information, exacerbating the effects of a high-choice media environment (Prior 2007).

Physical access to information only ensures the opportunity for exposure; individual-level motivations dictating audience selectivity and choice mean that exposure is not guaranteed (Stroud 2011; Napoli 2011; Arceneaux and Johnson 2013).

For example, the expansion of choice, via cable and internet proliferation, had the effect of providing physical access to more news channels, in more locations, at more times throughout the day. However, the opportunity for expansion was only realized by those with the motivation to consume more news (Prior 2007). Expanded access resulted in more news exposure for the most politically interested and the most partisan audiences; but the opportunity was lost on the uninterested. When the number of channels increased, people with little interest in political information had other options (Prior 2007; Arceneaux and Johnson 2013). The effect of the high-choice environment afforded by cable—despite the opportunity it provided for expanding access to public affairs information— was to widen the knowledge gap between those with political interest and those without, with the effect once again shifting the balance between breadth and depth of audience exposure to information. The high-choice environment meant that the breadth of exposure to news shrank to primarily include the politically interested (Prior 2007).

Our discussion so far suggests that changes in communication technologies can have important pre-exposure effects by altering the information available to people. They can change the delivery of content in ways that impact audience reactions to the content, changing the nature of exposure. The existing literature focuses a lot on what changes to the media environment (at least up through the arrival and proliferation of cable and the internet) meant for selectivity and its impact on the likelihood of exposure to particular kinds of information. However, an exclusive focus on physical access, choice, and exposure obscures learning about the way information is processed once exposure occurs, during what we refer to as post-exposure. While altering the structure of the market-place might be the most significant effect of the arrival of cable and broadcast, more recent changes in communication technology are altering the presentation of content in ways likely to constrain cognitive access to information.

POST-EXPOSURE EFFECTS

Extant work from several fields tells us a great deal about how communication technology can impact information processing. We will start by outlining what we know about the path through which exposure occurs and ultimately, how it shapes post-exposure information processing. *When exposure occurs, it is through one of two processes—motivated or accidental* (Prior 2007; Arceneaux and Johnson 2013), *with potentially distinct effects on cognitive access* (McGuire 1968; Zaller 1992; Kunda 1990; Grabe et al. 2000a; Arceneaux et al. 2015).

Since the earliest days of work on media effects and information process-ing research showed that: mediated communications have little or no effect on more deeply entrenched attitudes (Iyengar 2017; Jamieson 2017), due in part to audiences' ability to select (Iyengar 2017; Jamieson 2017), avoid (Festinger 1962; Stroud 2011; Arceneaux et al. 2015), or discount (Kunda 1990) information, and that political viewers are more likely to be exposed to political information due to interest but are less likely to be persuaded due to pre-existing attitudes and beliefs (McGuire 1968; Zaller 1992). The implication is that mere exposure to media messages is necessary but not sufficient to produce effects— individual-level traits, such as political interest, awareness, and predispositions, dictate both the path of exposure to information and the ease with which it is processed (Zaller 1992). Those that are motivated by their exposure to media messages may react differently to information once exposure occurs, relative to those incidentally exposed. Motivated people are more likely to be exposed, but they are most equipped to avoid or counter-argue the information when it is non-congenial. However, when they encounter information that they perceive to be neutral or agreeable it is processed more easily due to interest in and experience with politics. Those who are exposed to information incidentally may have reduced cognitive access upon exposure due to lack of interest or challenges in processing due to lack of familiarity with political information (Zaller 1992). Technologically imposed constraints on content may differentially affect those who are exposed through motivation relative to those exposed incidentally.

Message content and structure affect cognitive access because they influence the ease with which information is processed (Soroka 2014; Grabe et al. 2000a; Kunda 1990; Festinger 1962; Stroud 2011; Arceneaux et al. 2015), *suggesting that communication technologies affect cognitive access by shaping: (1) message content, and (2) message structure.* Research on information processing spans several decades and disciplines and made numerous advances in how we understand constraints on attention, learning, and knowledge in the face of exposure to political information. The various theories and frameworks converge on a key point: humans have limited capacity for attention (Lupia and McCubbins 1998; Lang 2000). Because attention is a finite resource, attending and processing political information is costly (Downs 1957; Lupia and McCubbins 1998; Lang 2000), especially for those with low political knowledge and interest, for whom processing political information is made additionally costly by lack of enjoyment, interest, or familiarity with the topic (Downs 1957; Lupia and McCubbins 1998; Lang 2000).

The very human traits making us inclined to behave as cognitive misers also make us more attentive to particular kinds of information. For example, negative news attracts more attention than positive or neutral news (Soroka 2014). People prefer and tend to remember negative information better, relative to information that is positive or neutral, because such information often has more utility from a psycho-evolutionary perspective (Soroka 2014; Trussler and Soroka 2014). The tendency to behave as cognitive misers also means that we avoid cognitive dissonance by mitigating the effect of counter-attitudinal information (Festinger 1962) through avoidance or counter-arguing, for example (Garrett and Stroud 2014). At the same time, we are more attentive to information that is highly engaging, immersive, or transporting because it is easier to process (Green and Brock 2000).

New communication technologies can shape message content if they require different editorial selections. For example, television news stories typically contain less factual information relative to newspaper stories, and mobile displays of the Facebook news feed remove article summary information to preserve space on smaller screens (Searles et al. 2017). The amount and complexity of information will affect ease of cognitive processing. However, most technological effects occurring at the exposure stage have to do with how communication technologies alter the structure of information display and presentation, and these effects can also operate in tandem with elements of information content (Burrows and Blanton 2016; Grabe et al. 2003; Lang 2000; Hou et al. 2012; Settle 2018).

Communication technologies also affect cognitive access through their influence on message structure (Grabe et al. 2000a; Lang 2000; Settle 2018). Elements of media presentation can structure information processing by making the content less difficult to cognitively process or by making it more engaging (Grabe et al. 2000b). Structural components can exert effects by presenting information in ways that make cognitive processing easier or more emotionally arousing. Emotionally arousing content attracts attention and affects the allocation of cognitive resources for encoding (Newhagen and Reeves 1992; Bradley et al. 1992; Lang et al. 1995), storage (Lang et al. 1999), and retention (Newhagen and Reeves 1992; Lang et al. 1999, 2003). In television, for example, structural characteristics like production pacing, video graphics, and camera zooms and pans, have known effects on cognitive processing (Lang 2000). In print, characteristics like the order of presentation and narrative structure can affect attention, arousal, memory, and persuasion (Green and Brock 2000). Similarly, interactivity and realism in video games are related to outcomes associated with arousal, immersion, presence, persuasion, and recall (Hou et al. 2012; Burrows and Blanton 2016). Research spanning several fields demonstrates that the structure of messages influences how they are processed and that communication technologies structure messages in consequentially different ways (Detenber and Reeves 1996; Grabe et al. 2000a; Hou et al. 2012; Burrows and Blanton 2016; Settle 2018).

Cognitive access is a precursor to learning, knowledge, and persuasion. Numerous studies link self-report and physiological indicators of attention, emotional arousal, and cognitive effort with outcomes like recall, memory, learning, and persuasion (Bradley et al. 1992; Drew and Grimes 1987; Graber 1990; Lang et al. 1995, 2000; Zaller 1992; Grabe et al. 2000a; Burrows and Blanton 2016). Larger

screens for example are thought to produce more accurate recall among viewers because they arouse more emotion relative to the same content viewed on a
smaller screen (Detenber and Reeves 1996; Horton and Wohl 1956; Lombard
et al. 1997). Arousing messages elicit more information processing resources
and attention than calm messages (Lang et al. 1995, 1996). Emotionally arousing content also produces better recognition memory and free recall (Lang
et al. 1999; Lang et al. 1995), drawing researchers to the conclusion that the
"consequences of arousing messages improve the ability of viewers to gain information from viewing television news" (Grabe et al. 2000, 7). Research clearly
suggests that cognitive access as measured by attention, arousal, processing, and
resources is required for outcomes related to information gain. A summary of
these arguments is found in Table 2.1.

Applying the PCA Framework to Mobile

We began this book by asking how bodies of research focused on the same technology could arrive at such different conclusions about its impact. A review
of mobile research points to a familiar divergence in the literature on media
effects: a divergence rooted in a failure to distinguish between differences in
access and exposure, and exposure and attention. Decades before, researchers
made all sorts of assumptions about the possible democratic implications of a
new form of media with potential for immediate and vast access. The product
of those assumptions in early propaganda studies (see Elasmar 2017) was negative, suggesting that because people sought out information, they were exposed
to it and subsequently, paid attention to it. Assumptions underlying early hopes
regarding the democratizing potential of digital communication technologies
were similarly misplaced (Hindman 2009). We know now, however, that those
assumptions are wrong: for both learning and persuasion, access is not equivalent to exposure and exposure is not equivalent to attention. Instead, there are
specific conditions under which access produces exposure and exposure bears
attention.

As with earlier confusion on these points, the divergent perspectives on
mobile are a product of failing to make these distinctions (see Chapter 1 for more
discussion).[1] Painting with broad strokes, we can make a distinction between
physical access to information, which creates an opportunity for political news
exposure and constrains motivation to seek it, and cognitive access to information, which is conditional on physical access to information, ability, content, and
the display and delivery of information. The physical/cognitive access distinction is conceptually helpful, at least as applied to the case of mobile, but other
scholars have drawn similar distinctions. For example, Markus Prior's definition

Table 2.1 **Summary of arguments**

Arguments
1. Communication technologies condition media effects through two processes: (1) through pre-exposure effects on the information market, which structure opportunity and motivation for exposure by dictating the boundaries of *physical* access to information; and (2) through their effects on the structure of messages, which affects *cognitive* access—or the ability to process information, post-exposure.
2. Communication technologies govern physical access to information through equipment and infrastructures capable of disseminating information; this physical access is characterized by access and choice afforded by the proliferation of broadcast technology, cable, high-speed broadband, and wireless internet connectivity.
3. Physical access to information only ensures the *opportunity* for exposure. It does not guarantee exposure because of the individual-level motivations dictating audience selectivity and choice. When exposure occurs, it is through one of two processes—motivated or accidental—with potentially distinct effects on cognitive access.
4. Communication technologies condition cognitive access by shaping message *content* in ways that affect the difficulty with which it is processed.
5. Communication technologies condition cognitive access by shaping message *structure* in ways that affect the difficulty with which it is processed.
6. Cognitive access and its various components—attention, arousal, activation, cognitive effort—are important precursors for learning, knowledge, and persuasion.

of the "media environment" overlaps significantly with our use of physical access. The OMA framework separates the effects of opportunity (which has to do with physical access) from individual-level traits influencing motivation and ability. Broadly, one can distinguish between information access, exposure, and processing. Or, as we do, physical and cognitive access as two levels with distinct implications for pre- and post-exposure processes.

As we highlighted in Chapter 1, our primary theoretical and empirical focus is on post-exposure processing because data on smartphone proliferation and the literatures on post-broadcast and mobile media already make it clear that mobile is expanding physical access to information. Due to its portability and relative affordability, mobile is expanding access to more people than just those able to afford high-speed broadband subscriptions. And, because smartphone technology is inherently high-choice, it has predictable implications for both purposive and incidental exposure to news and political information. Like early versions of the internet, mobile compounds the effects of the expansion of choice by extending the high-choice media environment in terms of space and time. For those who have access, mobile provides the opportunity for exposure to political information in more places and more times throughout the day. Although we encourage more research on how mobile devices might shape media selectivity, we think the market-structural implications of mobile are relatively clear.[2]

Most important for our point is that applying the distinction between physical and cognitive access to the mobile case accomplishes three important goals. First, it provides resolution to the disparate findings with respect to the impact of mobile by showing that mobile can at once expand physical access to information even as it constrains cognitive access to information. Yet, we unequivocally maintain that mobile access is better than no access. Instead, the real hazard exists under conditions of replacement, where people are choosing (or are forced) to rely on mobile for access to political information above other forms. Similarly, expansion of access in places without previous access must be accounted for when considering the downsides of constrained cognitive access, as subpar access is better than nothing. Second, it provides a lens through which we can view this and other changes to communication technology. Third, it does both of these things in a way that allows conceptual and theoretical parity with the history of the research on media effects and information processing.

Expectations

PRE-EXPOSURE EFFECTS

The global proliferation of mobile is opening channels of information to unprecedented numbers of people around the world. As we shall see in the next chapter, the trends clearly suggest the potential for mobile communication technology to expand physical access to news and political information. Mobile communication technology is widely viewed as a low cost means to erase lingering global digital divides in ways traditional computers with high-speed internet cannot. In the next chapter, we examine these trends and offer a test of this expectation. We hypothesize that *mobile devices expand physical access to information* (see H1, Table 2.2).

EFFECTS ON POST-EXPOSURE PROCESSING

Evidence from several fields gives us reason to expect that both news seeking and attention are different on mobile devices. Certain activities are too complex for mobile devices (Ghose et al. 2012), especially those "requiring storage,

Table 2.2 **Summary of hypotheses**

Hypotheses	Chapters
H1. Mobile internet access expands physical access to information.	3
H2. Mobile devices reduce attention to information.	5, 8
H3. Mobile devices increase cognitive effort.	7
H4. Mobile-sized screens reduce attention and arousal.	6
H5. Mobile devices reduce recall.	7

space, time, and bandwidth" (Donner and Walton 2013, 5). Mobile internet use is relatively passive and superficial (Humphres et al. 2013; Napoli and Obar 2014) when compared to computer-based internet use. Mobile internet searches, for example, are based on fewer, less complex search terms (Napoli and Obar 2014); occur across fewer categories (Cui and Roto 2008); and mobile users tend to rely only on the first few returned results (Ghose et al. 2012). Not surprisingly, internet users are much more likely to use a computer instead of a mobile device to seek out complex information about health, employment, finances, and politics (Donner and Walton 2013).

Screen size should also affect attention paid to news. Larger screen sizes present media content differently than smaller screens (Kim, Sundar, and Park 2011), with variable psychological effects, both cognitive and affective (Detenber and Reeves 1996; Lombard 1995). Large screens are associated with a higher sense of arousal, presence, immersion, and realism (Kim and Sundar 2016, 45; also see Kim and Sundar 2013; Detenber and Reeves 1996; Lombard 1995; Reeves, Detenber, and Steuer 1993). Information processing is easier with larger screens because they have more capacity to transport users to a virtual reality and a sense of "being-there," which encourages heuristic processing. Smaller screens encourage systematic processing, which requires more cognitive effort (Kim and Sundar 2016).

If larger screens facilitate information processing, mobile devices should influence attention to news. For a significant portion of the public, attending to political news by any means is hard. The challenges are greater for people with little education or low levels of digital literacy. Consuming news on mobile devices is even more challenging, especially when compared to computers with larger screens. The information processing costs imposed by mobile devices lead us to expect that, relative to mobile users, computer users will pay more attention to news content. Thus, we expect that *attention to news, operationally defined as time reading news content, is attenuated on mobile devices* (see H2, Table 2.2).

As a second test of H2, we also examine attention to news links. While scholars and democratic thinkers are occupied with the implications of the changing news environment for the informed democratic citizen, the news industry is grappling with questions about audience engagement. News companies and outlets must demonstrate audience engagement in ways that speak to advertisers and shareholders, which often constitute metrics such as time on page, click-through rates, and unique visitors. Observable gains in the improvement of online advertising occurred only just in time for another sea change—the massive shift to mobile. The mobile features that interfere with attending to news content also affect attention to links, which is a precursor to engagement by news industry definitions (Pernice, Whitenton, and Nielsen 2015). Again, just like attention to news content, we expect that *attention to links for recommended related stories is reduced on mobile devices*. We also examine whether people notice links less, look at them less often, and for shorter periods of time on mobile devices.[3] We expect each to be negatively related to mobile device use.

EFFECTS ON COGNITIVE EFFORT AND INFORMATION RECALL

If mobile audiences spend less time on news stories, are they still learning as much from news? Reduced recall is another implication of our theory. It is also possible that information processing on mobile devices is simply more efficient and that less time spent on content is not indicative of lower rates of learning. On the other hand, if less time spent attending to news means less learning from news, it is important to understand precisely why audiences are less attentive and engaged on mobile devices and with what effect. We hypothesize that *mobile users spend less time reading news content and as a result, they recall less information than those reading on a computer* (see H5, Table 2.2). To get at the underlying mechanism of this effect, we also hypothesize that *cognitive processing is more difficult on mobile devices* (see H3, Table 2.2).

EFFECTS ON POST-EXPOSURE PROCESSING OF NEWS VIDEOS

Why is it that mobile devices require more cognitive resources to process information? We can shed some light on this by isolating the effect of screen size and by differentiating effects from information content and information structure. We hypothesize that skin conductivity and heart rate variability, alternative measures of attentiveness and arousal, will be lower for those consuming news on smaller screens (see H4, Table 2.2). We demonstrate replicability and robustness by using different physiological measures of interest and attention, varying the level of negativity in the content, and by switching to video news content (Soroka and McAdams 2012; Daignault, Soroka, and Giasson 2013; Soroka 2014; Soroka et al. 2016).

EFFECTS ON ENGAGEMENT METRICS: MOBILE NEWS IN THE WILD

Is there evidence of mobile constraints on news consumption in real world media behaviors among computer, tablet, and smartphone users? We use real-world computer and mobile web-traffic data from "the wild" to replicate the results from our quasi- and experimental studies. If mobile devices curb time spent reading or viewing news content and engagement with content, then we should see this reflected in web traffic patterns by device. We test this implication with a real-world test of H2 using post-exposure engagement metrics such as average minutes per visit and average minutes per visitor (Hindman 2011), expecting they will be reduced on mobile devices.

Conclusion

The juxtaposition between physical and cognitive access to information on mobile devices reflects a familiar truism in related research: changes in communication technology reflect trade-offs between breadth and depth of exposure to information. In its current fragmented state, the literature on mobile communication technology does not acknowledge this or provide a clear indication about its implications for media effects. Unsurprisingly, streams of research representing perspectives from numerous fields arrive at variable conclusions about the societal harms and benefits of mobile communication technology. We argue that these perspectives are more easily reconciled when we make the distinction between physical and cognitive access to information. Generally speaking, studies focused on how mobile technology affects physical access to information offer a positive account relative to studies focused on cognitive access to information. Our model reconciles these perspectives by illustrating that both the positive and negative consequences of mobile are accurate. Mobile technology has a positive impact on physical access to information, while at the same time operating to constrain cognitive access to information. Like communication technologies that came before, mobile is expanding the breadth of access to information while limiting the depth of exposure.

In this chapter, we offered a framework consistent with other theoretical accounts of information seeking and processing (Downs 1957; Lupia and

McCubbins 1998; Lang 2000; Kim and Sundar 2016), one that incorporates and connects both the pre- and post-exposure stages. In the next chapter, we explore the first set of implications of our model as it relates to mobile communication technology, beginning with the effect of mobile technology on physical access to information.

3

Mobile Effects on Access and Exposure

Rapid improvements in wireless technology and the global proliferation of mobile access to the internet are opening channels of information to unprecedented numbers of people around the world, leaving little doubt about the potential for such technology to broaden the scope of physical access to news and political information. In fact, there is such enthusiasm for mobile's capacity to improve education, information equality, and opportunity that it is widely viewed as a low-cost means by which to erase lingering global digital divides in ways computers cannot (Napoli and Obar 2014).

In the U.S., growing segments of the population are abandoning broadband subscription services opting to rely on wireless access and mobile devices for internet use in the effort to cut costs (Horrigan and Duggan 2015; Perrin 2019). Tablets are also replacing desktop and laptop computers in classrooms and school libraries around the country (Murphy 2014). In other parts of the world, tablets are replacing computers at internet cafes and libraries, which people without home access rely on for critical internet use (Donner and Walton 2013). Research in developing settings finds that mobile access generally improves inclusion, learning, economic development, and quality of life (Donner 2015).

However, as we argue in Chapter 1, the implications of these broad shifts in reliance on mobile access have not been exhaustively interrogated. There remains a debate as to whether mobile access is a sufficient replacement for high-speed internet access on desktop and laptop computers, or access to information through other more traditional forms of media (Napoli and Obar 2014; Mossberger, Tolbert, and Franko 2013). While the sufficiency of mobile access is a matter of some debate, it is clear when we examine rates of access by device that the process is best described by trade-offs. On the surface, differences in information access via mobile devices versus computers is one of breadth versus depth: we see again and again that a majority of news consumers are using

News and Democratic Citizens in the Mobile Era. Johanna Dunaway and Kathleen Searles, Oxford University Press. © Oxford University Press 2023. DOI: 10.1093/oso/9780190922504.003.0003

mobile platforms to access news, but that these same users are unlikely to engage deeply with information as evidenced by the short duration of their average visits. These differences are reflective of the distinction underscored in our physical and cognitive access (PCA) framework, in which people may have physical access to information via their smartphones, but this access is distinct from cognitive access, which is diminished on a mobile device. In Chapters 5 to 8, we will provide evidence that attention and information acquisition are curbed on mobile devices. But first, in this chapter, we will explore the extent to which mobile news consumption results in audience displacement—in which mobile devices replace or supplement information consumption—and the degree to which mobile technology is expanding access to information in the U.S. and globally.

The Shift to Mobile: Supplemental or Replacement?

Historically, concerns about audience displacement effects have been central to researchers' intense focus on the informational consequences of changes to communication technology (Gaskins and Jerit 2012). We know, for example, that the arrival of television meant the erosion of radio audiences (Bogart 1957), and that the array of channels provided by cable services depleted broadcast news audiences (Webster 2014). And while displacement patterns do not typically unfold rapidly or completely, evidence suggests new communication technologies tend to replace older technologies over time (Althaus and Tewksbury 2000; Gaskins and Jerit 2012).

Numerous studies suggest, for example, that the internet is replacing older forms of media as a source for news (e.g., Dimmick et al. 2004). Studies from the early 2000s reveal that the use of older, more traditional forms of media declined alongside increases in internet use (Dimmick et al. 2004; Stempel et al. 2000; Bakker and Sadaba 2008; Johnson and Kaye 2003; Waldfogel 2002). Other studies find replacement patterns occurring for only certain subsets of the public, such as among younger age cohorts (De Waal et al. 2005). In a more recent study, Gaskins and Jerit (2012) apply uses and gratifications theory to predict and explain replacement, finding nuanced patterns. Their analyses reveal that replacement is occurring, but it is not widespread. They identify important differences across forms of media and subsets of the public. For newspapers and radio, substitution and replacement patterns are strong; for television, usage patterns persist, even as internet use increases. Perhaps more important for the present discussion is their finding that people who replaced older communication

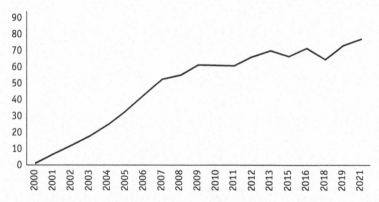

Figure 3.1 U.S. home broadband use over time, 2000–2021 Source: Adapted from Pew Research Center, Internet & Technology, Accessed July 22, 2021, https://www.pewresearch.org/inter net/fact-sheet/internet-broadband/#home-broadband-use-over-time. Data are from Pew surveys conducted between 2013–2021. Data for each year based on a pooled analysis of all surveys conducted during that year. Pew surveys with relevant broadband use questions were not conducted in 2014, 2017, or 2020.

technologies with the internet reported doing so because of its variety and convenience.

While not a focus of the authors, when it comes to mobile it is easy to imagine people replacing computers because of the convenience afforded by smartphones' portability. And, there is circumstantial evidence to suggest that replacement trends explain some mobile use in the United States. According to Pew, the percentage of U.S. adults with home broadband internet subscriptions dropped from seventy-three percent in 2016 to sixty-five percent in 2018 (see Figure 3.1) (Pew Research Center 2019). Though 2021 saw modest increases in rates of broadband adoption after a period of decline, smartphone adoption still outpaced that of high speed internet. Moreover, most of those who do not subscribe to broadband at home consistently report the high costs of high speed internet and computers as the reason (Perrin 2021).

Over the same time period, there was a corresponding twelve percent increase in the percent of U.S. adults reporting a smartphone as their primary means of accessing the internet (see Figure 3.2). In 2018, these smartphone-only internet users made up twenty percent of the U.S. adult population. Pew data also suggest replacement is not just about cord-cutting. Among the sixty-six percent of respondents who report consuming digital news on both computers and mobile devices, fifty-six percent report that they *prefer* to read news on a mobile device (Barthel 2016).

In light of the research (reviewed in Chapter 2) suggesting that mobile access does not reap the same informational benefits as high-speed access on

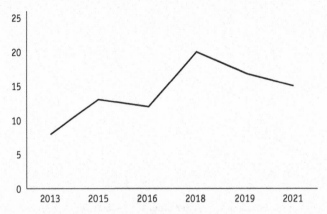

Figure 3.2 U.S. smartphone dependency over time, 2013–2021 Source: Adapted from Pew Research Center, Internet & Technology, Accessed July 22, 2021, http://www.pewinternet.org/fact-sheet/internet-broadband/. Data are from Pew surveys conducted between 2013–2021. Data for each year based on a pooled analysis of all surveys conducted during that year. Pew surveys with relevant smartphone questions were not conducted in 2014, 2017, or 2020.

traditional computers, these patterns raise questions about the implications of smartphone dependency for an informed citizenry. In 2015, for example, mobile-only Pew respondents reported the decision to cut broadband service as a major impediment to keeping up with the news. Similarly, research shows that high-speed internet in the home is a major determinant of online news-seeking while mobile access is not (Mossberger, Tolbert, and Franko 2013).

Mobile Access and Information Inequities

The consequences posed by changes in communication technology raise concerns about whether the effects of such changes vary systematically across groups, especially when they have the potential to exacerbate existing information inequalities (see Figure 3.3). Looking again at the U.S. case, shifting reliance on smartphones seems poised to do just that. Latinos and African Americans make up the two largest groups of smartphone-only internet users, at thirty-five percent and twenty-four percent, respectively. The number of smartphone-only users in both groups has grown since 2016, but the percentage of Latinos has grown by twelve percent.

Smartphone dependency also varies by income, education, urban/rural residency, and age. Only nine percent of American households earning $75,000 or more per year rely on smartphones for access, while thirty-one percent of households earning less than $30,000 annually are wireless only (see Figure 3.4). Almost forty percent of people without a high school degree report relying on

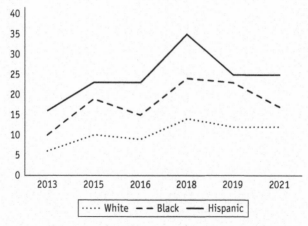

Figure 3.3 U.S. smartphone dependency by race and ethnicity, 2013–2021
Source: Adapted from Pew Research Center, Internet & Technology, Accessed July 22, 2021, http://
www.pewinternet.org/fact-sheet/internet-broadband/. Data are from Pew surveys conducted between
2013–2021. Data for each year based on a pooled analysis of all surveys conducted during that year.
Pew surveys with relevant smartphone questions were not conducted in 2014, 2017, or 2020.

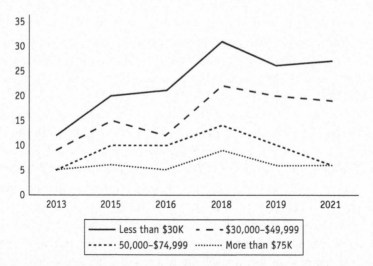

Figure 3.4 Smartphone dependency by income, 2013–2021 Source: Adapted from Pew
Research Center, Internet & Technology, Accessed July 22, 2021, http://www.pewinternet.org/fact-
sheet/internet-broadband/. Data are from Pew surveys conducted between 2013–2021. Data for each
year based on a pooled analysis of all surveys conducted during that year. Pew surveys with relevant
smartphone questions were not conducted in 2014, 2017, or 2020.

wireless access, while ten percent of those with college degrees are smartphone
reliant. A higher proportion of people living in rural and suburban communities
are also more likely to depend on smartphones access to the internet at seventeen
percent; only twenty-two percent of urban residences are mobile dependent.

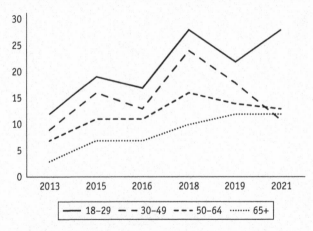

Figure 3.5 Smartphone dependency by age, 2013–2021 Source: Adapted from Pew Research Center, Internet & Technology, Accessed July 22, 2021, http://www.pewinternet.org/fact-sheet/inter net-broadband/. Data are from Pew surveys conducted between 2013–2021. Data for each year based on a pooled analysis of all surveys conducted during that year. Pew surveys with relevant smartphone questions were not conducted in 2014, 2017, or 2020.

When smartphone dependency is broken down by age, we see an increase in the overall trend across groups, but more pronounced rates of reliance on mobile phones in younger users (see Figure 3.5). Indeed, about twenty-eight percent of respondents aged 18–29 are dependent on their smartphones for internet access (Perrin 2021).

When we shift our perspective globally, it is clear that in some parts of the world wireless access to the internet is needed to fill the gap. South Africa, for example, has one of the lowest rates of high-speed broadband penetration, whereas smartphone ownership is at fifty-one percent. Similarly, broadband penetration is low in Turkey, reaching only between six and fourteen percent of the public, while smartphone ownership is at sixty-nine percent (Pew 2019; World Bank 2019). According to World Bank (2019), about 12.5 of every one hundred people have high-speed broadband subscriptions around the world, and the global median for smartphone ownership is fifty-nine percent (Pew 2019). As depicted in Figure 3.6, it is clear that smartphones and wireless tech-nologies are expanding global access to the internet.[1]

These data suggest that significant portions of citizens around the world are heavily dependent on wireless technology and mobile devices for access to the internet. Although mobile access to the internet is certainly preferable to none, the data also suggest that any informational effects we observe from the use of mobile devices will have a disproportionate effect on some segments of the public, both domestically and globally. Despite the importance of these patterns of displacement, it is also important to examine mobile's reach more

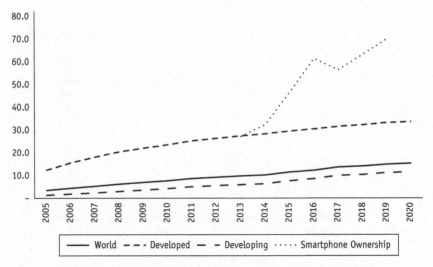

Figure 3.6 World broadband subscriptions and smartphone ownership, 2001–
2020 Source: Broadband data are from The International Telecommunication Union (ITU) 2005–
2020 ICT data, https://www.itu.int/en/ITU-D/Statistics/Pages/stat/default.aspx. Smartphone
data are from Pew Research Center Global Attitudes Surveys from Spring 2017 and Spring 2019. Pew
smartphone data from 2016 are missing for Indonesia, Philippines, South Korea, Vietnam, Israel,
Jordan, Lebanon, Tunisia, Turkey, Ghana, Kenya, Nigeria, Senegal, South Africa, Tanzania, Argentina,
Brazil, Chile, Colombia, Mexico, Peru, and Venezuela, inflating percentages for that year.

generally, even among those for whom mobile supplements other modes of
access. How often is digital news consumed on mobile devices relative to computers? And how much? If audience reach through mobile devices is as broad as
these data suggest, any important differences in attention across these formats is
consequential.

Breadth versus Depth: Mobile and Audience Reach

We start with some basic descriptive evidence showing important tendencies in
mobile use based on Comscore web-traffic data for well-known national news
outlets. Comscore provides proprietary web traffic data, and a rare glimpse into
people's real-world consumption habits. These data include one-quarter of a million internet users, and with them we are able to examine patterns in usage and
reach on smartphones and tablets compared to computers.[2] Figure 3.7 shows
the average number of minutes that visitors spend on selected major news sites
by mode of access (desktop computer, mobile web browser, or mobile app).
Figure 3.8 shows audience reach by mode of access; audience reach is defined as
the percentage of the total internet audience that sites reached.[3]

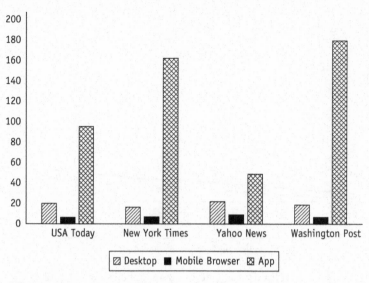

Figure 3.7 Average visitor minutes spent on selected news sites Source: Data are from Comscore, Media Metrix Data for March 2016.

As Figure 3.7 shows, attention to news as defined by time on news sites is quite high among mobile users who use news apps. In fact, time spent on sites via mobile app exceeds the time spent on sites via desktops or mobile web browsers. In light of what we know about Americans' preferences in a high-choice media environment, these statistics are predictable. Only those with the highest levels of political interest will download news apps on their mobile devices. We can expect them to pay substantial attention to mobile-delivered news. Yet, they are relatively few in number, as Figure 3.8 shows.

The mobile news app audience is only a fraction of the desktop or mobile-browser audience. Most mobile users encounter news content through web browsers, much of which is the result of referrals from social media sites like Facebook (Messing and Westwood 2014; Collier, Dunaway, and Stroud 2021).[4] Figure 3.7 also shows that time spent on sites via desktops is more than double that of the time spent via mobile browsers. Another look at Figure 3.8 points to a breadth versus depth of exposure trade-off. Although mobile browser users' average time on news sites is short—mobile provides the greatest audience reach.

To look at this data another way, we use the same data to model predicted audience reach by device. Figure 3.9 shows predicted values for audience reach by mode of access. While these values are generated for browsers-only, the results are the same when we include apps (see Appendix). When we model predicted audience reach, we see evidence that substantially more of the digital media audience is being reached on smartphones relative to computers. Despite

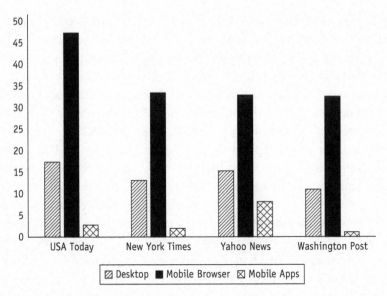

Figure 3.8 Percent internet audience reached Source: Data are from Comscore, Media Metrix Data for March 2016.

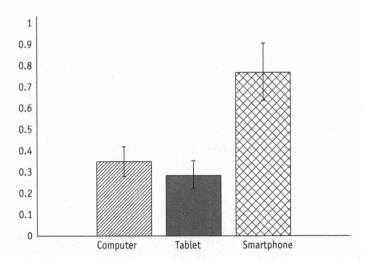

Figure 3.9 Predicted percent audience reached with 95 percent confidence intervals, by device (Study 5) Source: Data are from Comscore, Media Metrix Data for March 2016.
Notes: Predicted values are generated for users accessing news sites via web browsers. See Model 1 in Table A3.1 of the Appendix.

the growth in tablet sales and the pervasiveness of computers, these reach patterns are not altogether surprising given that far fewer people have tablets than smartphones and that our analyses include computer web traffic from both home and work. Tablet audience reach is likely suppressed by its typical use as a supplemental means of web access and that far fewer people have tablets relative to smartphones. Audience reach via computers for media sites is likely constrained by the fact that so many people using a computer to access media content must do so between tasks required for work or school, at least during business hours (Boczkowski 2010). Nevertheless, at more than double the reach of computers and tablets, the pervasive reach of smartphones is clear. For full models, including model with apps see Tables A3.1 and A3.2.

The breadth versus depth trade-off is also apparent in the Pew Research Center's analysis of the top fifty digital news sites. Most of the top fifty news sites keep visitors on their desktop sites for longer average visits relative to mobile, and yet, most of these sites also had more mobile visitors (Pew 2016).

The Pew data also show that most outlets' traffic consists of mobile visitors. People are accessing websites using their mobile devices at high rates, but most are not spending very much time on those sites on average. Recent data from Adobe Analytics echo these findings, showing a huge uptick in smartphone web-traffic, stagnant growth in visits through computers and tablets, and a steep decline in app launches (Molla 2017). Figures 3.10 and 3.11 illustrate these trends.

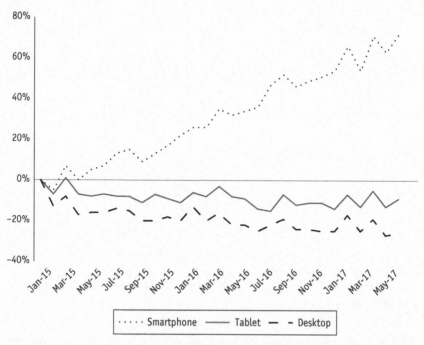

Figure 3.10 Change in U.S. website visits, by device Source: Data are from Adobe Analytics. Figure is adapted from, Molla, R., Smartphones are driving all growth in web traffic: Just not through apps, *Recode*, September 11, 2017, https://www.recode.net/2017/9/11/16273578/smartphones-goo gle-facebook-apps-new-online-traffic.

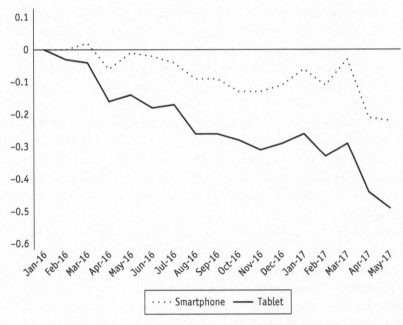

Figure 3.11 App launch declines for smartphones and tablets Source: Data are from Adobe Analytics. Figure is adapted from, Molla, R., Smartphones are driving all growth in web traffic: Just not through apps, *Recode*, September 11, 2017, https://www.recode.net/2017/9/11/16273578/smartphones-google-facebook-apps-new-online-traffic.

Taken together, these patterns of use indicate a breadth (audience reach) versus depth (time spent on site) trade-off: breadth is better on mobile devices, and for smartphones in particular, but attention is more substantial on computers. These data reflect a familiar pattern—differences in communication technologies shift the cost of information seeking and the balance between breadth and depth of exposure.

Conclusion

Patterns of use evident in the web traffic data illuminate the trade-offs inherent in the shift to mobile. While these data point squarely to the consequences mobile devices have for breadth over depth, they also offer support for our PCA framework: mobile represents a trade-off between physical and cognitive access to information. Much of the mobile digital news audience uses smartphones to only minimally engage with content. As a result, although many more people reach news sites through smartphones, these visits are significantly shorter than the visits of those on computers.

What's more is that growing segments of the U.S. population either entirely or mostly rely on mobile-only internet access (Horrigan and Duggan 2015). There is a critical difference between mobile-only internet use and supplemental mobile internet use. For those who have high speed internet access through a computer at home, the information gathering constraints that characterize the mobile environment are not as consequential. For these people, the affordances of mobile devices can be deployed strategically—when portability and ease of use is important—while computers can be used for difficult tasks like in-depth searches. But access to high-speed internet subscription services varies significantly by geography and demography, exacerbating existing information inequities as defined by the quality of access (DiMaggio and Hargittai 2001; Lelkes 2020).

Our descriptive analyses with Comscore data suggest that attention and engagement with news is relatively fleeting on mobile devices when compared to traditional computers. They also suggest that these effects are especially stark for smartphones, which are the most widely used for internet access. Yet, at this point we cannot definitively answer whether physical access to mobile devices limits cognitive access to information. We tackle this question in Chapters 5 to 8.

The web traffic data provided in this chapter offer behavioral measures that tell us something about how mobile technology affects the breadth of physical access to information. Measuring cognitive access is much more difficult, requiring a toolkit that allows for more precision, as well as the control afforded by experimental design. Because our methods are somewhat unconventional, we introduce and describe them in detail in the next chapter.

4

Studying Technological Change and Media Effects

Chapter 3 highlighted the value of observational data for illustrating how emerging communication technologies effect access and exposure to mediated information. These data show that mobile communication technology is expanding physical access to information. Even in the U.S., where high-speed internet penetration is relatively high, the proportion of the public relying on mobile devices for news is growing, and this is especially true for informationally disadvantaged subsets of the population.

But as the discussions in Chapters 1 and 2 suggest, the balance of post-broadcast literature on media effects largely focuses on how changes to the market affect audience behaviors, with consequences for the frequency and nature of exposure. *What remains understudied in this post-broadcast era is how new communication technologies constrain information processing once exposure occurs.* The imbalance makes sense given the expanded access and choice afforded by today's information environment, changes widely regarded as having profoundly reshaped the contemporary information environment (Prior 2007; Bennett and Iyengar 2008; Stroud 2011; Arceneaux and Johnson 2019). This body of work provided critically important and increasingly sophisticated insights into how information available in the marketplace shapes media selection and exposure (Benedictis-kessner et al. 2019).

Nevertheless, this disproportionate focus on selectivity, choice, and exposure is reaching the point at which it is slowing broader theoretical progress for media effects. The digital media environment makes it easier for researchers to know who is exposed to what information on what platform or website, and on what device, but very little work tells us anything about how those devices and platforms constrain whether that information is attended or processed—both of which are necessary conditions for media effects. The challenge of this post-broadcast era is to understand how the proliferation of communication

News and Democratic Citizens in the Mobile Era. Johanna Dunaway and Kathleen Searles, Oxford University Press. © Oxford University Press 2023. DOI: 10.1093/oso/9780190922504.003.0004

technologies is changing the way mediated messages are communicated, with repercussions for information processing. This requires advancing the literature on mobile communication technologies and the broader literature on media effects to go beyond the study of how changing media technologies affect exposure to the study of how they affect *post-exposure information processing*. However, methodological limitations frequently challenge these efforts; properly measuring the effect of communication technology on information processing requires the use of a different methodological toolkit.

Paying Attention to Attention (And How to Measure It)

Historically, studies of media effects faced challenges to accurately measuring media exposure (Bartels 1993; Prior 2009), media attention (Chaffee and Schleuder 1986; Bode 2016; Caplin 2016), and ostensibly related outcomes such as information recall, learning, and political knowledge (Jerit et al. 2013; Barabas et al. 2014). News exposure is particularly hard to measure with self-reports. Respondents consistently over-estimate and over-report their news exposure and consumption (Prior 2009, 2012; Jerit et al. 2016). As a result, scholars are moving to passive measures for capturing exposure to news (Ohme et al. 2016; Nelson and Lei 2018).

Despite these advances, improving the measurement of media exposure solves only part of the problem. Exposure is necessary, although not sufficient, for capturing attention. Exposure provides only the opportunity for attention. A person may be exposed to media messages because they are in a room with the television on, but those circumstances do not guarantee attention. This distinction between exposure and attention is why, despite their wide use, ratings based measures are insufficient for capturing attention and other forms of audience engagement.

MEASURING ATTENTION

Early scholarship in psychology, political science, and communication recognized the importance of capturing attention (Schattschneider 1960; Riker 1962; Kingdon and Stano 1984). Social psychologist William McGuire (1968, 179) put attention at the center of an information processing approach to persuasion, arguing that attention—while hard to operationalize—was central to reception and comprehension of a message. Tackling this hard-to-measure concept, Chaffee and Schleuder (1986) use political knowledge questions as an external criterion for attention, in addition to self-report attention and exposure.

What the literature reveals is that—for a host of reasons—people are too often unable or unwilling to accurately report their media exposure, much less the degree to which they pay attention to particular elements of media messages. The problems associated with self-reported exposure make it clear that media effects research cannot rely solely on self-report measures. Yet despite much discussion about problematic measurement, most recent research on media effects has not made use of an array of psychophysiological methods and measures relied on in earlier media effects work, as well as in other fields. (For notable exceptions see Soroka 2014; Soroka and McAdams 2015; Vraga et al. 2016; Bode et al. 2017; Bode and Vraga 2018; Vraga et al. 2019.)[1]

Early work on television, for example, used psychophysiological methods to better understand the effects of changing television set size on audience responses to media content. Lombard and his colleagues (1997) reported more intense responses to content displayed on larger screens. Physiological studies demonstrated more heart rate deceleration among viewers of large screens relative to those watching medium and small screens, indicating higher levels of attentiveness; skin-conductance was higher for large screens, indicating more arousal (Reeves et al. 1999). In psychology and human–computer interaction, studies manipulated screen size to show how it shapes content display, affecting audiences' feelings of immersion and transportation (Thompson et al. 2012; Rigby et al. 2016). Such findings are important because when text or video messages successfully transport audiences into a feeling of "presence" or "being there," they process messages with more ease relative to less-transported audiences (Green and Brock 2000; Sundar 2008; Kim and Sundar 2014, 2016; Burrows and Blanton 2016), another aspect of cognitive access. Despite these important insights and the promise of these tools for capturing attention and other effects from exposure, research in media effects has only intermittently made use of psychophysiological measures to understand attention and reactions to media messages (Potter and Bolls 2011).

PSYCHOPHYSIOLOGY IN STUDIES OF MEDIA EFFECTS

Here we draw on several insights from the previous literature on information processing and media effects to help make the case for our use (and the broader use) of psychophysiological measures for understanding how communication technologies shape media effects. The first is that information processing perspectives elevate the role of physiological systems. The second is that processing is dictated by both automatic and controlled responses to media exposure. The third is that psychophysiological measures are the most appropriate approach to capturing automatic/unconscious responses to media messages in real-time. We offer some background on our approach, and each of the psychophysiological methods that inform it.

OUR APPROACH

McGuire (1968) wrote decades ago that attention was required before persuasion could take place. This remains true, and applies to more than just persuasion. Attention is vital to understanding all media effects in a digital, social, and mobile media age. However, as discussed above, the complex and elusive nature of attention means methodological concerns must inform design. In other words, we must pay attention to attention. To put our model to the test, in subsequent chapters we will demonstrate there are differences in attention and engagement across devices and then posit evidence for the mechanisms underlying these differences.

First, we pay special attention to several methodological challenges that plague the measurement of media effects. Deficiency in the reliability and validity of self-reported measures is an ongoing challenge in media effects research (Prior 2009, 2012). To combat these issues, we use physiological measures in addition to survey measures, including galvanic skin response and eye-tracking technology. Specifically, use of such measures allows us to circumvent self-report issues related to attention to news, which is very difficult for people to recall accurately.

Second, our model poses that consuming information on a mobile device is costly, and that such costs are captured in the high cognitive demands demonstrated by people using their smartphones to read, for example. The long literature on political participation points to two important kinds of information-seeking costs (e.g., Downs 1957; Riker and Ordeshook 1968). In the present theoretical context and given the evidence cited in Chapter 1, we focus on costs in terms of cognitive demands. Accordingly, we argue that cognitive demands shape the effects of mobile technology on learning. Thus, to test for our causal mechanism, we use an experimental approach to discern differences between treatment groups on a physiological measure (either pupillary response, heart rate variability (HRV), or skin conductance levels (SCL)) which indicates cognitive demands have been recruited to execute the task. For this mechanism test, advances in eye-tracking methodology are particularly useful. Pupillary responses provide the means by which we can simultaneously observe the amount of visual attention paid to specific pieces of information, and the cognitive demands required to process the information.

To isolate the relationship between mobile devices and differences in cognitive access, we use a series of experiments. In addition to leveraging the logic of experimentation, this allows us to exploit the strict internal validity afforded by lab experiments to ensure differences in aspects of cognitive access, like attention, can be attributed to the treatment, or in this case, use of a mobile device. We summarize our basic experimental approach in Figure 4.1.

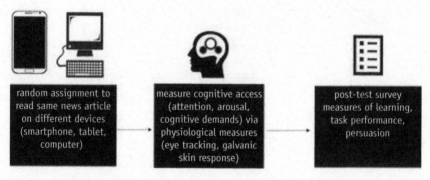

| random assignment to read same news article on different devices (smartphone, tablet, computer) | measure cognitive access (attention, arousal, cognitive demands) via physiological measures (eye tracking, galvanic skin response) | post-test survey measures of learning, task performance, persuasion |

Figure 4.1 Experimental approach to understanding how mobile devices affect information processing

While experiments with student participants are appropriate for testing psychological mechanisms when we expect them to be the same in adult populations, it is useful to triangulate using different data sources, methods, and samples. To this end, and to shore up external validity, we also employ a quasi-experiment using adult participants from an online labor market. In this study (Study 3), we ceded control over assignment to condition and asked the participants to take the survey on whatever device they preferred. This allows us to detect whether effects persist when people read news articles under more natural circumstances and using the device of their choice.

To maximize treatment equivalency in all experimental studies, the appearance and format of content is the same across devices. To create the stimuli for the experiments in Studies 1 to 3 a former news reporter edited actual news stories (see Figures 4.2 to 4.4). In Experiment 1 the news article focused on pay equity, and in Experiment 2 the news article focused on Donald Trump's appearance on NBC's *Saturday Night Live*. In Experiment 3 we used two articles as stimuli, the first was a news article focused on pay equity, the other was an entertainment-oriented story focused on the possibility of a television sitcom reboot. For each stimuli, the text was crafted to resemble a basic online news article. Each article included hyperlinked articles in the footer using the heading "Related Stories" to detect whether or not a participant noticed a link to the article. The links were drawn from actual related articles and were not live. Aside from differences in story focus, the only key difference between stimuli across the studies is that the stimuli in Study 2 featured a photo.

Our fourth lab study uses news videos to extend these results to different medium (video news stories), and includes within-subject variation in story tone and interestingness. Participants viewed seven news stories, on a range of topics, political and otherwise. Of the seven stories, one was domestic and negative, and one was domestic and positive. The remaining five were drawn from a sample of eight international stories, four positive and four negative. The

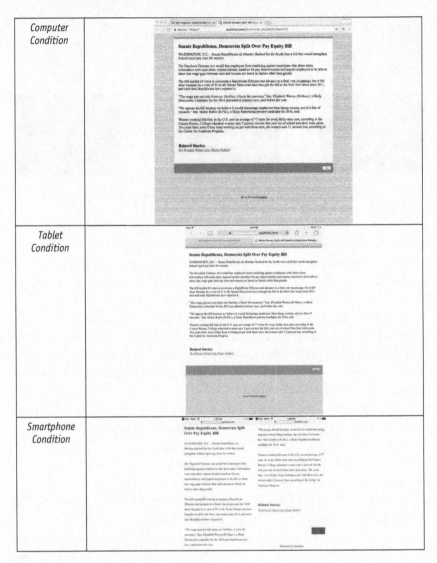

Figure 4.2 Study 1 stimulus by condition

(non-random) sample of articles consists of carefully selected real news stories from BBC World News presented in a random order, first preceded by two minutes of grey screen, and then separated by 40 seconds of grey screen. The stories are listed in Table 4.1 below (for more details see the Appendix). In the last column is tone, as indicated by the binary measure based on second-to-second codes by researchers and expert coders.

Our fifth study uses cross-sectional analyses with passively tracked web-traffic data from a national sample of adults. As the appropriate measure of attention is central to our broader argument regarding media effects in a mobile age,

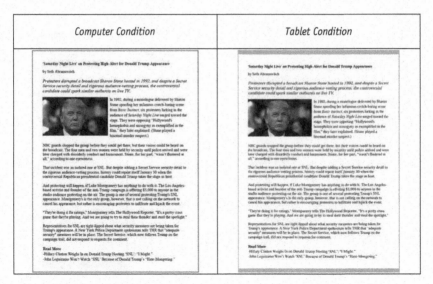

Figure 4.3 Study 2 stimulus by condition

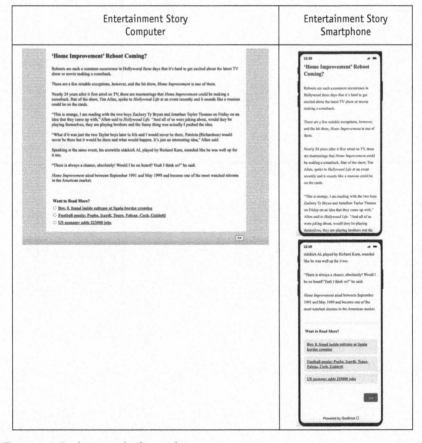

Figure 4.4 Study 3 stimulus by condition

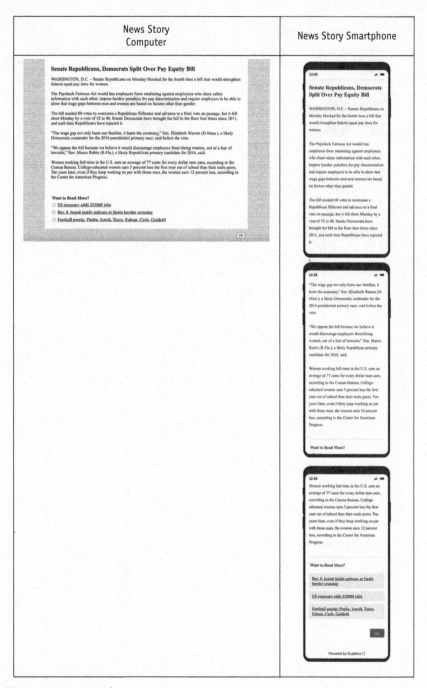

News Story Computer	News Story Smartphone

Figure 4.4 Continued

Table 4.1 **Video stimuli (Study 4)**

Title	Description	Tone	Mean Neg	
			Experts	Participants
International				
Peru	Small town of Chimbote burns down	negative	1.122	4.710
May Day	May Day protests following economic downturn	negative	0.855	3.400
Niger	Food shortages in Niger	negative	1.082	4.857
UN Sri Lanka	UN investigations in war crimes in Sri Lanka	negative	1.258	5.107
Gorillas	Gorillas are released into wild	positive	−1.031	1.645
Folding Car	New electric, folding car intended to reduce congestion	positive	−.347	1.383
Young Director	Eleven-year-old makes stop-motion films	positive	−1.017	1.095
Cured Liver Disease	Young child recovers from liver disease	positive	−.570	1.508
Domestic				
Homeless	A homeless man in downtown LA is battered and shot by police	negative	1.080	5.752
Bagpipes	A U.S. man learns how to make bagpipes	positive	−.6723	1.208

we discuss in greater detail our physiological measures next. A summary of our empirical strategy is presented below in Table 4.2. We also present additional methodological details in the Appendix.

EYE TRACKING

Eye tracking captures what content participants are attending to and for how long. It is a well-tested measure of visual attention and cognitive processing (Duchowski 2007; Vraga et al. 2016). Eye-tracking technology is used for research in many domains, from human–computer interaction to psychological. It is also used by web designers for functional purposes, as well as for diagnostic uses by patients with physical and speech impairments. While a variety of

Table 4.2 **Overview of empirical approach**

Study	Sample	Stimulus	Dependent Measures
Study 1 Eye tracking experiment Chapters 5 and 7	Student subject pool	Online news story	*Attention* to news story/links captured with eye tracking: time fixated on news content, duration of fixations on links, counts of link fixations, whether links were noticed at all. *Cognitive effort* captured with eye-tracking measure of pupil dilation. *Recall* measured with post-test survey items.
Study 2 Eye tracking experiment Chapters 5 and 7	Student subject pool	Online news story	*Attention* to news story and links captured with eye-tracking measures of time fixated on news content, duration of fixations on news links, counts of fixations on link, and whether links were noticed at all. *Cognitive effort* eye-tracking measure of pupil dilation. *Recall* measured with post-test survey items. *Sustained recall* measured twenty-four hours after treatment delivery.
Study 3 Quasi-experiment Chapter 7	Online labor market (Amazon Mechanical Turk)	Online news story	*Attention* to news story and links measured with time on page. *Recall* measured with post-test survey items.
Study 4 Psychophysiological experiment Chapter 6	Student subject pool and adults	Video news stories	*Attention* to news videos measured with heart rate variability. *Emotional arousal* to news videos measured with skin conductance levels.
Study 5 Observational study Chapters 3 and 8	Comscore web traffic data for news websites		*Audience reach* captured with Comscore measure of percentage of total internet audience reached. *Attention* to news captured with Comscore measures of average minutes per website visit/visitor.

systems exist, trackers generally capture aspects of gaze as an observable measure of visual attention. Attempts to measure visual attention by examining the human gaze date back more than one hundred years (Huey 1908). Given that we are interested in both whether and how mobile devices affect information processing, we use eye tracking to create a measure of attention duration outside of participant awareness, or the time participants were looking at the body of the news story. We also use eye tracking to create a measure of cognitive effort, or significant pupil dilation, during exposure to the stimulus.

We use eye trackers in two lab studies (see Chapters 5 and 7) to capture visual attention to the same news article by device (tablet, smartphone, computer). Eye trackers capture several outcomes of interest—where people look, the order in which they look, for how long, and pupillary response (dilation of pupil). In our model, we treat how long people look as an indicator of visual attention, and pupil dilation as an indicator of cognitive effort (Wang et al. 2010). Eye tracking offers more reliable measures of attention (Duchowski 2002, 2007; Pan et al. 2004; Bode et al. 2017) than self-reported measures (for a discussion see Graham et al. 2012; Vraga et al. 2016).

Eye trackers use a combination of projectors and sensors to capture the position and gaze direction of a user's eyes using near-infrared light, unaffected by ambient light conditions. This setup allows for freedom of head movement for the comfort of participants. In conditions using a computer, we employ an internal Tobii T120 eye tracker to record eye movement at 120 Hz on a 17-inch monitor with a screen resolution of 1280 x 1024. The T120 relies on a binocular, automatic tracking optimization technique to ensure accuracy and precision of measurement. The eye tracker is covertly integrated into an otherwise normal looking desktop, allowing for detailed stimuli. In mobile device conditions (tablet and smartphone), we employ an external Tobii X260 eye tracker attached to a docking station to which an iPad 2 (9.5 x 7.31 inch) or iPhone 6s (4.7 x 5.5 inch) records eye movement at 60 Hz (see Figure 4.5). This difference between internal and external eye-tracking units is out of necessity. To eye track mobile devices, the only alternative is to have participants wear headgear, which is far more obtrusive and less externally generalizable.

For all conditions we use the Tobii Studio 3.2 software suite to manage the collection and export of data. Tobii Studio 3.2 records a variety of outcome measures, but for our purposes we use fixation duration and counts and pupil size. Fixations filter out blinks and pass-through eye movements (e.g., saccadic movements) to indicate thoughtful, focused visual attention. Tobii uses a mathematical filtering process to ensure fixations are identified consistently, indicating visual processing. Fixation duration indicates how long a person spent attending to a given visual element. Fixation counts indicate how many times a person fixated in an *a priori* established "Area of Interest" or AOI. AOIs allow

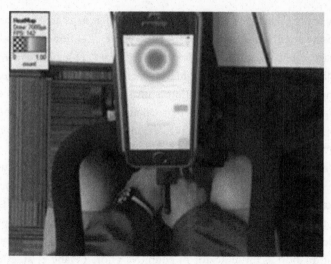

Figure 4.5 External mobile docking setup for eye tracking experiments Notes: External
Tobii X260 eye tracker attached to a docking station for iPad 2 (9.5 x 7.31 inch) or iPhone 6s
(4.7 x 5.5 inch), used in mobile device conditions (tablet and smartphone).

the researcher to isolate and analyze data from specific areas of screens, pages, or
content that are relevant, such as news story text or an image, rather than including visual attention from the margins around the relevant material. Given the
immense amount of data eye tracking offers, recording both eyes movements
every few milliseconds, it is important to focus the analyses. News title, each
paragraph of the story, and the links were coded into separate areas of interest
(see Figure 4.6). Fixation duration and fixation counts are used to capture attention per our model (see Table 4.2).

Pupil size is also measured using the eye tracker. Recall that our model asserts
mobile devices impose cognitive costs on users, in the tradition of political information seeking more generally (Downs 1957; Riker and Ordeshook 1968).
Using pupillary responses (changes in pupil size), we isolate the effects of device
on effort, showing differences in the cognitive effort associated with consuming
information on a computer or mobile device. When engaging in a task, such as
reading a news article, pupils dilate in response to cognitive demands (Beatty
1982; Chatham et al. 2009). Pupillary responses measure the influence of central nervous system processing in a task. Decades of research demonstrate the
efficacy of pupillometry in the examination of cognitive processes (Beatty and
Lucero-Wagoner 2000), and pupillary response consistently predicts task complexity across a variety of stimuli (Beatty 1982).

Upon assignment to a device condition, participants were instructed in a nine-
point calibration procedure to ensure valid measurement of eye movements.
Participants were recalibrated if necessary. Participants were then informed that

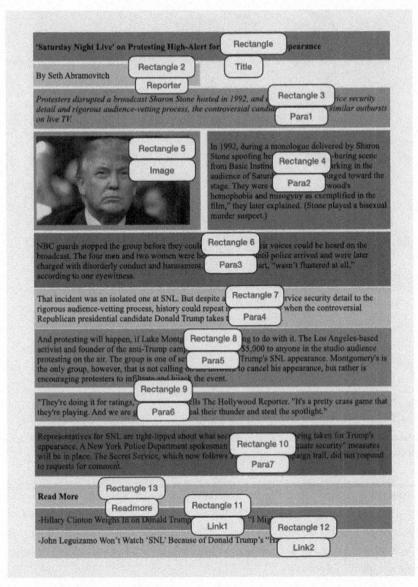

Figure 4.6 Areas of interest (Study 2) Notes: "Area of Interest" (AOIs) designated for Study 2, using Tobii eye tracking software. Story title, reporter name, the image, each paragraph of the story, and the embedded links were coded into separate areas of interest.

next they will see a news article that they should read at their leisure, at which point the stimulus appears within the browser and their eye movements are recorded. There was no time limit on the eye-tracking procedure; when finished participants moved back to the original desktop computer for the post-test. Pupil size, fixation duration, and fixation counts for each AOI per participant were

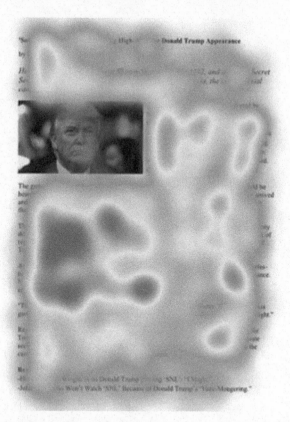

Figure 4.7 Visualizing duration of participants' fixation on stimulus Notes: Image depicts a heat map displaying the variation captured with eye tracking using our actual stimuli from Study 2; the darker areas indicate longer average fixation durations.

exported and analyzed using Stata SE 13. Because respondents were identified by a unique ID number, we matched eye-tracking data with the responses from each respondent. Figure 4.7 provides a visual of the variation captured with eye tracking using our actual stimuli from Study 2; the darker areas indicate longer average fixation duration.

SKIN CONDUCTANCE LEVELS AND HEART RATE VARIABILITY

Following earlier research on information processing and media effects (Bolls et al. 2001; Bucy and Bradley 2004; Detenber et al. 1998; Simons et al. 1999), recent work on the effects of negative news (Soroka 2014; Soroka and McAdams 2015; Soroka et al. 2019), and the use of psychophysiological measures in research in politics and communication more generally (Schreiner et al. 2019; Soroka 2019; Carlson et al. 2020), we rely on psychophysiological indicators of activation and engagement in Study 4. Much like eye tracking, these measures permit us to avoid problems with inaccuracies in self-reported data on exposure to media (Boase and Ling 2013; Bolls et al. 2019; Kim and Capella 2019; Prior 2009; Settle et al. 2020; Wagner et al. 2015). To be clear, we do not hold the position that self-report data are inaccurate; indeed, psychophysiological methods are often highly correlated with self-reports, but relying solely on self-reports can produce an incomplete picture (Prior 2009). The research enterprise can benefit from researchers triangulating across data types (MacDuffie et al. 2019; Settle et al. 2020).

Our approach draws considerably from the literature on news engagement, both with respect to news content and platform (Barreda-Ángeles et al. 2020; Kulta and Karjaluoto 2016; Nelson and Webster 2017; Nelson and Lei 2018; Schreiner et al. 2019), and where screen size is concerned (Detenber and Reeves 1996; Lombard et al. 2000), as well as the extant literature on information processing and media effects (Grabe et al. 2000b). We focus on cognitive access, which we regard as a precursor to information processing, recall, memory, learning, persuasion (Grabe et al. 2000a; Yoon et al. 1998), and one that is appropriately operationalized with SCL and HRV. We expect information displays on smaller screens to induce lower rates of attentiveness and arousal as captured by HRV and SCL.

SCL are intended to capture arousal, or activation. HRV is intended to capture some combination of activation and attentiveness. The use of variability reflects the fact that heart rate tends to decrease with heightened attentiveness, but also increase with arousal, and HRV captures the variance produced by these countervailing effects. There is a sizeable skin conductance literature in communication, and our interpretation of SCL and heart rate is consistent with this past work (e.g., Bolls et al. 2001; Bucy and Bradley 2004; Detenber et al. 1998; Lalmas, O'Brien, and Yom-Tov 2014; Marci 2006; Peacock et al. 2011; Rúas-Araújo et al. 2016; Simons et al. 1999; Soroka 2019; Soroka et al. 2019).

In this study, HRV and SCL are measured while participants watch a series of news stories. Participants are given noise-canceling headphones and assigned a computer in a quiet room. They then completed the survey online in the same lab. Critically, each participant is assigned to either the a large- or small-screen treatment group, meant to mimic the differences between computers and mobile devices. Large- and small-screen treatments were identical in every way, except for the size of the window displaying the video (i.e., all participants watched the video on the same size laptop but the size of the video varied), which was either the size of a large laptop screen (roughly 13 inches wide), or the size of standard smartphone screen (roughly 4.5 inches wide). Note that this is a relatively small difference—past work focused on screen size has tended to compare very small (i.e., 12-inch) with very large (i.e., 46-inch) television screens (Lombard et al.

2000). Given that our aim here is to compare differences in attentiveness and arousal across different online mediums, however, we use this comparatively small shift in screen size (smaller even than the shift to a large desktop monitor). This should make statistical significance across treatments more difficult to attain.

There are several ways to measure HRV, and we rely on two in Study 4: (1) the standard deviation of the NN intervals (SDNN), calculated over each news story, and (2) the Root Mean Square of the Successive Differences (RMSSD); that is, the square root of the mean squared differences of successive NN intervals. We calculate both across all seven stories, excluding the inter-stimulus intervals.

We capture activation using SCL, measured using sensors attached to the first and third fingers on participants' non-dominant hand. We focus on the mean of "normalized" SCL across all seven stories, where "normalizing" SCL involves measuring all stimulus-period SCL relative to SCL during each prior inter-stimulus interval. This serves to remove variation in skin conductance across individuals, so that analysis focuses on change in SCL from before to during the video stimulus. Higher normalized SCL is taken to indicate greater levels of arousal.

In addition to the basic SCL measure, we explore a measure that captures variation in SCL across positive and negative video. Recall that we regard this more as a measure of attentiveness than arousal—SCL captures arousal, to be sure, but here we capture the extent to which arousal varies systematically with video tone. This is critical for our tests.

MEASURING ATTENTION IN THE WILD

As always, the use of lab experiments raises questions about external validity. Sensitive to this concern, we conducted two additional studies designed with the particular aim of addressing what we view as the primary threats to validity in our lab-based experimental designs. The first is that the artificiality of the experimental setting may influence the manner in which participants engage with content; the second is that random assignment to device conditions, while necessary, is a forced-choice design as it may require participants who to consume news on a device they would not choose.

In Study 3, we address these concerns about whether the patterns we see in our lab experiments replicate across samples and in other contexts. First, we use a quasi-experiment embedded within a web-based survey on an adult sample recruited through Amazon's Mechanical Turk (MTurk) platform. Unlike our lab experiments, this design permits participants to use the device of their preference, which we categorize as mobile (tablet and smartphone) and computer.

To ensure we accurately captured the device used, we triangulate across participant's self-reported device use, Qualtrics embedded data on device, and a picture-based method to proxy differences in content displays by mode, allowed for by subtle color differences in Qualtrics default mobile display and the display on our desktops and laptops. Studies of media effects are often criticized for low levels of external validity, such as a failure to allow for media choice. Here we are able to improve on external validity by allowing participants both media choice and device choice. This extension of our lab work is important because it is likely that participants who use their device for an MTurk study are also likely to use these devices for news consumption.

Participants selected either a news article on pay equity or an entertainment article on a reboot of the television show *Home Improvement*. After reading the story they chose, participants answered questions about the article aimed at capturing what they recalled. We also capture time reading the story, via Qualtrics, to approximate our lab attention measures.

In Study 5, we use web traffic data from Comscore to again address external validity concerns. Comscore is a cross-platform measurement company that provides website level data to quantify consumers' multiscreen behavior. Comscore keeps monthly web traffic tracking data among computer, tablet, and smartphone users for around six thousand websites and apps worldwide.

We can use these data for real world tests of our attention hypotheses. In the world of web traffic, the outcomes conceptually and theoretically closest to our lab measures of attention to news are indicated by the total minutes users spend on news sites, and how much time users spend on the page once there.

The media world is structurally complex, and the Comscore data measure multiple categories of media companies and their various web domains, including channels, sub-channel, group, subgroup, custom entity, media, property, and so on. Because Study 5 focuses on audiences' engagement with news media via different devices, our analysis draws on media-level data only. Comscore defines sites at the "media" level as "an editorially and brand consistent collection of content in the digital landscape that provides the marketplace with a view of online user behavior. This may represent a domain, a group of domains, online service or application" (Comscore 2016, 2). This measurement, akin to how we might think of a "media outlet" or "news brand" is automatically documented by Comscore, so we employed it to draw a dataset that includes sites (websites and apps) at this level only.

Next, we enlisted a trained coder to classify sites in the sample as providing content that was either news, entertainment, both, or neither.[2] We then collapsed the data into a dichotomous indicator for whether the site provides news versus entertainment content. Afterward, to ensure a comparison across desktop, tablet, and smartphone users, we computed a dummy variable to capture whether an outlet is available on all three devices, dropping those that did not. This cuts the units of observation for analysis to 3,285, which captures individuals' engagement with 1,300 media websites via desktop, tablet, and smartphone.

We use these data to estimate models clustered by news outlet to predict average minutes per visitor and average minutes per visit. Where the number of observations permit, we model both browser and app users. These data provide tests of our hypotheses using unobtrusively measured digital news consumption behavior in the real world. We report additional details and the findings from Study 5 in Chapter 8.

Conclusion

In a mediated world characterized by pop-up ads, never-ending news feeds, and constant notifications it is important to understand how people attend to information across platforms and devices. The news industry in particular, which faces an increasingly noisy and fragmented news environment, finds itself in the unenviable position of attention merchant, seeking and finding new ways of attracting and retaining audience attention. Because of contemporary levels of mobile proliferation, news outlets must now compete for our attention around the clock, even as we are on the go, flitting through the distraction of daily routines.

That media is increasingly divorced from modes of distribution makes distinguishing between the two a difficult task. In the current media environment, it is not just information content that is monetized, but the time and energy required to secure attention (Webster 2014). Unlike the broadcast era, in which advertisers could be more confident their audience was watching one of three shows during primetime hours, today the question of *how* people consume information is at the core of media in the digital age. Answering this question necessitates an accounting of attention. Marketing models *begin* with attention. This is where we begin, too.

Today, purchasing online ad impressions quantifies eyeballs on ads, monetizing attention potential in a way heretofore unseen (Benkler 2006). But buying power does not guarantee attention, as distribution of content is fragmented between outlets and dispersed between modes. In other words, while accessibility and proliferation characterize today's marketplace, reach and cognitive engagement with information in this market structure is unclear. For example, a news article published by a legacy newspaper will also be pushed to nontraditional modes such as digital media, in controlled ways (republished by the newspaper's site online) and in uncontrolled ways (reposted by a political blogger). And thus, the question of who saw the article—much less who paid attention to it and for how long—is more complicated than ever. While a challenge for industry, this changing digital media context makes measuring attention both more difficult and more important. Moreover, in the context of media effects, differences in attention may explain the heterogeneity of responses when exposure is held constant.

And still, there are very real limits—limits we argue *should* inform the study of news consumption on mobile devices. While news is now accessible whenever, wherever, the number of hours in our days remains the same. Attention is a limited resource (Webster 2014), and we still know little about how its allocation shapes news consumption on mobile devices. As such, we seek to understand whether, given what this "poverty of attention" (as Herbert Simon [1971, 41] referred to it) means for the move to mobile. In this way, like most political tasks, we can think of consuming news on a mobile device as an endeavor delimited by attention supply (Webster 2014) and structured by bounded rationality and the costs that motivate satisficing (Simon 1971). Research on visual attention provides evidence for this approach, demonstrating that when people encounter stimuli in their environment they engage in habitual processing to direct their attention efficiently (Chen et al. 2008).

While the methods have varied, one thing is clear: to account for attention, scholarly investigations must begin to analyze how the features of platforms and devices affect individuals' ability and willingness to pay attention to information, or what we refer to as cognitive access. In this book, we focus on a particular case that presents unique challenges information processing, mobile devices. Noting the importance of attention to understanding how mobile devices shape the way we process information, as well as the difficulty in measuring attention, our empirical approach uses multiple methods, including measures taken outside of participant awareness, to ensure robust and reliable results. We use several physiological methods, eye-tracking, HRV and SCL, to capture a range of attention measures including pupillary response, duration of visual attention, number of fixations, attentiveness and emotional arousal, in addition to survey measures of learning. Balancing methods in and out of the lab, we leverage the affordances of experimental approaches when testing our theory, extending these results to the real-world using adult and convenience samples.

5

Attention to News on Mobile Devices

WITH MINGXIAO SUI AND NEWLY PAUL

Digital news consumption has dramatically shifted to tablets and smartphones. In 2021, sixty percent of U.S. adults—up from just twenty-one percent in 2013—said they often get their news on a mobile device; a mere thirty percent said they often get their news on a desktop or laptop computer (Shearer 2021). This pattern is not surprising given precipitous increases in mobile device ownership in the United States. A majority—eighty-five percent—of Americans report owning a smartphone (Perrin 2021). Tablet ownership increased from just three percent in 2010 to fifty-one percent in 2021 (Perrin 2019). Among smartphone owners, ninety-four percent report carrying them frequently, rarely turning them off (eighty-two percent), and using them several times a day (fifty-nine percent) or constantly (twenty-seven percent) (Rainie and Zickhur 2015). A full fifteen-percent of American Adults are smartphone dependent for internet use (Pew 2021).

For the remainder of the book, our goal is to assess the ways in which mobile devices structure attention and learning, and the consequences of these effects for an informed democratic electorate. In this chapter, we examine how the use of mobile devices for news consumption shapes attention to content. Our investigation is motivated by evidence that suggests mobile devices are overtaking desktop computers as the primary vehicle for consuming digital news (Mitchell et al. 2016; Newman et al. 2017), as well as evidence underscoring the limitations of mobile platforms for news consumption (Kim and Sundar 2014, 2016; Molyneux 2017; Napoli and Obar 2014).

News and Democratic Citizens in the Mobile Era. Johanna Dunaway and Kathleen Searles, Oxford University Press. © Oxford University Press 2023. DOI: 10.1093/oso/9780190922504.003.0005

Mobile Exposure to Information: Paying Attention to Costs

Before we do this, we recall the model introduced in Chapter 2. In previous chapters, we argue that physical access to information is a necessary but not sufficient condition for attention to news. Neither access nor exposure are equivalent to attention because we are cognitive misers; attention is a finite resource only allocated on an as-needed basis, depending on individual utility calculations (Redlawsk 2004). Our theory is based on a rich literature on civic and political participation which builds on this logic, showing that the likelihood of engaging in participatory behaviors is constrained by perceived costs and benefits (Downs 1957; Riker and Ordeshook 1968; Zaller 1992). According to this view, information seeking by any means is defined as a costly endeavor. Research on user experiences and mobile communication technology suggests we can think about the effects of mobile communication technologies in the same way—in terms of how it affects information-seeking costs for users. Evidence from several fields lends support to the supposition that consuming news on a mobile device is costly relative to doing so on desktop computers (Napoli and Obar 2014). This logic is apparent in the application of our model to mobile devices, which posits that mobile technology shapes message structure in ways that make information processing more difficult. Our model is built on the premise that we cannot assume news seeking opportunities and consumption experiences afforded by mobile devices are the same as those afforded by computers. Yet, available evidence does not yet reveal how attention and engagement are affected by mobile devices. There are industry and usage trends that are suggestive, but the evidence is limited because it generally does not speak to effects regarding the normatively important category of news. Next, we offer several expectations regarding how the mobile setting curbs news attention.

Mobile Effects on Attention

ATTENTION TO NEWS CONTENT

For a significant portion of the public, attending to political news is an effortful task, and the cost of information seeking is viewed as a deterrent to civic engagement. The time and attention required by political participation exerts a cognitive tax and incentivizes "rational ignorance." In this calculus, information costs are considered against the benefits of becoming informed (Downs 1957). Ostensibly, the same calculations apply in the digital information environment. As the perceived costs of information seeking on mobile devices increase, the likelihood that users are willing to expend precious attention on news decreases.

When modes of content delivery make information seeking and attention more effortful, such as the need to scroll or find specific information, the costs may outweigh the benefits for all but the most dedicated democratic citizens (Zaller 1992). The implications should be reflected in the way people consume news on mobile devices.

Information-seeking costs have always been considered in terms of both cognitive and time constraints (Downs 1957; Lupia 1994; Zaller 1992). The effort required for information seeking and processing is compounded by the features of mobile devices, relative to computers with larger screens and the functionality of traditional computing platforms. Here we focus on how mobile devices affect information processing. We expect that mobile users will spend less time, relative to computer users, thoughtfully processing news content. Therefore, mobile users should spend less time reading news content relative to computer users. Put simply, our second hypothesis (see H2, Table 2.2), is that *mobile devices reduce attention to information.*

ATTENTION TO NEWS LINKS

As we argue in Chapters 1 and 4, the contemporary media environment demands new and different ways of measuring news attention. Historically, the methodological challenges associated with accurately measuring attention meant that the news industry often focused on measures that approximated the number of eyeballs reached. But things have changed. Today, the media industry has access to more precise measurement tools that can reveal who has their television sets or radios tuned to what (Napoli 2011). Importantly for our purposes, these measurement capabilities, such as pages viewed and time spent on page, allow for more precise measurement of post-exposure processes (Napoli 2011). These measures of exposure are critical to contemporary news organizations and their advertisers. They offer the best means to capture audience engagement and are also important precursors to the consumer behaviors of interest to digital advertisers, like clicks on embedded links and ads. These metrics are widely viewed as the future of the digital media marketplace (Napoli 2011).

Recommended news links often follow an article on news websites and are offered to provide additional information of relevance to the consumer, and more importantly for the outlet, in efforts to keep someone on the site. The economic logic is obvious: more visitors mean more eyeballs on ads, while more clicks mean more time spent on site and more time engaged with content and ads. Thus, whether news audiences pay attention to links is important in today's media environment, especially as a struggling news industry looks to maximize audience share. Attention to links, like other audience metrics, such as time on page, demonstrates audience engagement in ways that speak to advertisers and shareholders. We contend that the same constraints that prohibit attending to news content also affect attention to links. Moreover, investigating differences in attention to links by device allows us to test an industry-relevant measure, and provides an alternative conceptualization of attention to news content to test H2. Drawing on these arguments, we expect that, as H2 suggests, *attention to news links is also reduced on mobile devices.*

Mobile Attention Experiments

In this chapter, we test H2 using two pretest–posttest lab experiments featuring eye-tracking technology (see Chapter 4 for more details). Experiments are ideal for testing our hypotheses because experimental methodology affords us great control over delivery of the news content we are interested in tracking, or the "treatment." Such control means that we can isolate the mechanisms at work in shaping differential attention outcomes by device. More simply, we can randomly assign people in two groups to the same conditions, only varying the device or machine on which they read the news article. Randomization ensures that the two groups are comparable in composition. The benefit of this approach is that we can infer any differences in attention paid to a news article on a computer versus the attention paid to a news article on a smartphone are attributable to the device. This ability to speak to cause and effect makes experiments a popular method for inquiries in the realm of media effects and information processing.

Each experiment examines the effects of mobile devices on attention to news content and news links. Results from Study 5 (see Chapter 3) suggest that attention to news content and links is significantly different across computers, smartphones, and tablets. Chapter 4 provides additional methodological information and an overview of our experimental approach (see Figure 4.1). We recruited a total of 171 students for two different lab studies, and randomly assigned them to read a news article on either a smartphone, tablet, or computer. Our sample was on average 20 years old, white, Republican, and female, as is often characteristic of university samples (for exact demographic breakdowns see Table A4.1).

In the second study, we narrow the focus of our experiment to tablets and computers. This afforded us the ability to focus our analytical power on a more conservative test. Thus, Study 1 featured three treatment groups (tablet, smartphone, computer) and Study 2 featured two treatment groups (tablet, computer). In both studies, the appearance and format of the news article was the same for each group (see Figure 4.2-4.4 for visuals). This design allowed us to estimate the effects of reading news on a mobile device versus reading news on a computer. Participants first answered some basic demographic and political interest questions in a pre-test before reading the news story on their assigned device. Before exposure to the story, everyone read a statement advising them that an article was to follow and that they should take their time reading. Following exposure to the news article, participants answered recall questions, the results of which we present in Chapter 7.

In this chapter, we focus on eye-tracking measures for attention to content and attention to links to test H2. The *Computer* condition employs a desktop with an internal eye tracker. The *Tablet* and *Smartphone* conditions employ an external eye tracker setup (see Figure 4.5 for a visualization of the setup).

Because we want to test whether exposure to information on a mobile device affects attention to content and attention to links, we used eye-tracking data to capture visual attention to the news article. This approach is superior to measures such as time on page, which can capture amount of time the page was open, but not how much time attention was focused on the content of the page. In contrast, the eye tracker can tell us whether individuals are looking at the screen, which section of the screen is the subject of focus, and extraneous eye movement from focused visual attention. For example, an eye tracker helps us to discern between thirty minutes on a page actually reading the article, and thirty minutes on a page because the person is staring into space.

We used the eye trackers to capture four indicators of visual attention in order to test H2. The first, *Reading Time,* captured the total amount of time participants spent fixating on the body of the news story, which was six paragraphs long. We capture attention to recommended links at the end of a news article using several different measures including *Duration of Fixations on News Links,* which measured the summed duration of all fixations on the links; *Counts of Fixations on Links,* which summed the number of times a participant fixated on the link; and finally, *Noticed Links,* which measured whether participants looked at the link at all. The results we present here are robust to alternative model specifications, including reading speed effects.

In Study 1 we modeled these outcomes as a function of two predictors, *Tablet* and *Smartphone,* with the comparison category *Computer.* We estimated the effects of mobile devices on user attention to the news story and linked content by regressing treatment indicators on four outcome variables. The results are shown in Figure 5.1 with ninety-five percent confidence intervals; full models for this and other figures can be found in the Appendix. A significant and negative coefficient for *Tablet* and *Smartphone* indicates, as H2 suggests, that people in the *Tablet* and *Smartphone* conditions spent significantly less time reading news content relative to computer users. And because use of the eye tracker enabled us to capture thoughtful visual attention, we know that this significant time deficit for people in the *Tablet* and *Smartphone* groups translates to less attention to news content on those devices.

Turning to the results for attention to links presented in Figure 5.2, we see a similar pattern of results. For each model, ninety-five percent confidence

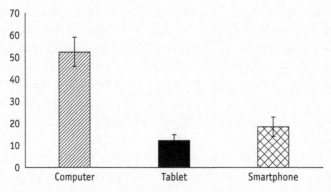

Figure 5.1 Predicted time spent reading news content (in seconds) with 95 percent confidence intervals, by device (Study 1) Notes: Predicted values correspond to Model 1 presented in Table A5.1 of the Appendix. Time spent reading news content is measured by number of seconds participants fixated on the body of the news story.

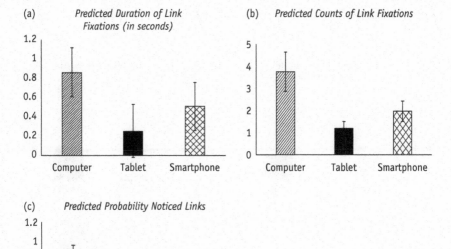

Figure 5.2 Predicted attention to News links with 95 percent confidence intervals, by device (Study 1) Notes: Predicted values in top left panel correspond to Model 2 presented in Table A5.1 of the Appendix. Predicted values in top right panel correspond to Model 3 of Table A5.1; predicted values in the lower panel correspond to Model 4 of Table A5.1.

intervals are displayed with the exception of *Predicted Counts of Link Fixations*, which displays standard errors. *Tablet* and *Smartphone* are significant and negative predictors of *Duration of Fixation on News Links, Counts of Fixations on Links*, and *Noticed Links*. These results suggest that people reading on tablets or smartphones spend less time paying attention to news links, look at news links less, and are less likely to notice links at all, relative to people who read on computers. Altogether, these results support H2, which suggests that when people read on tablets and smartphones, they pay less attention overall.

As noted previously, there is one critical difference between Study 1 and Study 2: in Study 2 we drop the smartphone condition. Briefly, focusing on the *Tablet* and *Computer* conditions permits us to make better (and more conservative) inferences given lab constraints. Additionally, there was no significant difference in any of the four outcomes for tablets or smartphones in Study 1. Otherwise, in Study 2 we take the same steps but focus on the *Tablet* and *Computer*, estimating the effects of tablets on user attention to news and linked content by regressing treatment indicators on the same four outcome variables. The results are shown in Figure 5.3.

For each model displayed in Figure 5.3, ninety-five percent confidence intervals are displayed with the exception of *Predicted Counts of Fixations on Links*,

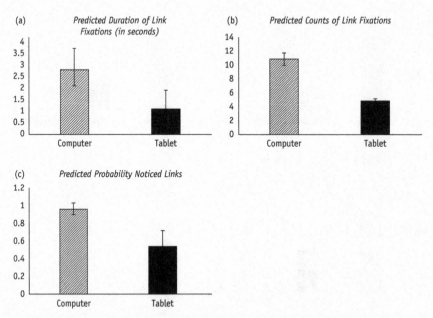

Figure 5.3 Predicted attention to news links with 95 percent confidence intervals, by device (Study 2) Notes: Predicted values in top left panel correspond to Model 2 presented in Table A5.2 of the Appendix. Predicted values in top right panel correspond to Model 3 of Table A5.2; predicted values in the lower panel correspond to Model 4 of Table A5.2.

which displays standard errors. We do not observe the significant and negative effect of *Tablet* on *Reading Time* replicate in Study 2. However, the data again yield significant and negative coefficients for *Duration of Fixation on News Links, Counts of Fixations on Links,* and *Noticed Links,* showing again that people assigned to read the news article on the tablet were less likely to look at recommended links and if they did, looked at it less often and for less time.

Discussion

Drawing on our model of post-exposure processing, in this chapter we test hypotheses about whether the mobile setting curbs attention to news content and news links and argue it does this by making information seeking costly on these devices. H2 posits a negative relationship between mobile device use and time reading news; it is supported in Study 1 where we find differences in duration among both tablet and smartphone users. Next, we examine the relationship between mobile device use and attention paid to links in a news story. Results show that mobile device users are less likely to fixate on news links and do so for less time, relative to computer users. In Study 2, we replicate tests of news attention from Study 1. With the exception of time spent reading the news content, Study 1 results are supported.

These results have important implications for democracy and the news industry. If mobile devices begin to replace, rather than supplement, other means of news consumption, the proliferation of mobile devices may do more than bridge lingering digital divides. Our results suggest that the story of mobile access is more nuanced. For many, mobile technology expanded physical access to news and political information by expanding access to the internet, providing more opportunity for exposure. But mere exposure does not equate to attention. Attention—an important precursor for learning—is curbed on mobile devices because they constrain cognitive access to information. This means that even as the breadth of information access—the breadth of audience reach—is growing through mobile access, for those who rely heavily on mobile, the depth of attention to news is shrinking.

Conclusion

In this chapter, we test H2 using two lab experiments with eye-tracking technology. Eye tracking affords us the opportunity to examine how people visually attend to news content and news links, while our methodological approach allows us to draw inferences regarding mobile device effects on attention. Across both studies, attention to links, measured several different ways, was attenuated for people reading on tablets or smartphones. In Study 1 this attenuating effect extended to attention to news content overall, although we did not see this relationship replicate in the more conservative Study 2 test. Overall, when people consume information on a tablet or smartphone, they are likely according less thoughtful attention to content with repercussions for learning. We tackle this possibility in Chapter 7.

6

Psychophysiological Responses
to Mobile News Videos

WITH STUART N. SOROKA

As we argue in previous chapters, even if it is the case that mobile technology facilitates widespread *physical* access to information, the constraints it imposes on *cognitive* access make for a more limited information seeking and processing experience. The evidence we present in Chapter 5 suggests this to be true, and while it is robust, our eye-tracking experiments are limited in a few important respects. First, they focus on text forms of digital news content, leaving open the question of whether our findings generalize to video news content. Second, they do not tell us about how the effects of mobile devices may vary according to differences in news story content, such as variations in tone. In this chapter, we address these limitations with a lab experiment in which participants view video news stories, under either large- or small-screen conditions, using an experimental design that also allows an exploration of whether screen size effects vary by story tone.[1]

The experiments presented in this chapter differ from those in Chapter 5 in four key ways. First, here we use online video news stories as our stimuli, rather than text-based stories. This difference in medium helps to mitigate any concern that the results from Chapter 5 may be driven by text-specific challenges for a small screen, such as the density of information per screen display or scrolling.

Second, we completely isolate the effect of screen size by conducting the entire experiment on laptops and varying only the dimensions of the window in which the video news story is shown. In other words, unlike Chapter 5 where text treatments are delivered on either a smartphone, tablet, or computer, in this chapter the only difference in display of the video treatments is size of the viewing window. This approach reduces the possibility that differences between computers and mobile devices (including the angle and distance of device from the face) are driving the effects we observe.

Third, we also vary the tone of stories within-subjects. Because motivations to attend news stories vary greatly according to the characteristics of those stories, we account for the potentially arousing nature of stories by coding them for positive and negative tone, and this sentiment coding is critical to ensuring that the effects we observe in our other chapters are not an artifact of the interesting or uninteresting nature of the news story stimuli, and because previous work shows the important effects news story tone can have on audience cognitive and emotional engagement (Soroka 2014; Soroka and McAdams 2015).

Finally, we switch to a different set of unobtrusive indicators for measurement of our key outcome variables. Here we define cognitive access operationally with psychophysiological indicators, as either heart rate variability (HRV) or skin conductance level (SCL). Both are known indicators of attentiveness and arousal and are widely interpreted as being reflective of information processing (Soroka 2019). SCL is intended to indicate activation, or arousal, while HRV is intended to capture some combination of activation and engagement. We introduce this change to reassure skeptics that our findings are not an artifact of our methodology. In line with existing work in the field, we view both arousal and attention critical to cognitive access and as important precursors to learning from public affairs news (Grabe et al. 2000a).[2] Our expectations are straightforward: we expect heightened engagement with content (as indicated by attention and arousal) to be indicated by increases in SCL and HRV and we expect that SCL and HRV will be lower when news is viewed on a smartphone-sized screen.

In summary, each difference in the design is aimed at accomplishing one of two things: (1) to ensure that our main finding—that mobile devices limit attention—is not an artifact of news format, the use of eye tracking, story type, or tone; and (2) to isolate the effect of screen size as a primary mechanism for the effect. In this chapter we test H4, which posits that mobile-sized screens reduce attention and arousal (see Chapter 2 and Table 2.2 for more details). We first motivate our hypothesis by drawing on literature looking at structural influences on information processing. Then, leveraging our unique research design, we discuss the link between content effects and structure. This expansion on H4 lends robustness to our argument that communication technologies structure cognitive access by shaping message content *and* structure (see Table 2.1). Using both HRV and SCL, our findings suggest that screen size limits cognitive access to online video news, and even more so for negative online video news.

Screen Size and Information Processing

STRUCTURAL EFFECTS ON INFORMATION PROCESSING

Early work on the effects of screen size emerged either in response to technological change, for example the changing size of television sets, or as part of a general interest in how people process information in text, relative to still and moving images (Lombard et al. 1997; Grabe et al. 1999). In recent years, work on screen size has been motivated by the growing proliferation of smartphones (Kim and Sundar 2014, 2016). These studies underscore the importance of screen size for information processing.

Foundational work examining the effect of screen size on physiological arousal also points to the importance of screen size for audience responsiveness. Larger screens are consistently associated with greater physiological arousal relative to smaller screens (Detenber and Reeves 1996; Lombard et al. 1997; Lombard et al. 2000). Early work on screen size shows its effects across several domains of audience response: perceptions of reality and presence, enjoyment, arousal, attention and memory, evaluation, and intensity of response (Grabe et al. 1999). Less is known about how screen size interacts with features of media content (or the context in which exposure occurs) to shape responses to content (Grabe et al. 2003)—and we consider one feature of media content, negativity, in the section that follows. Independent of content, however, the implication of past work is clear: small screens structure information displays in ways that restrict cognitive access. Relative to small screens, large screens are better at creating a virtual reality, which is reflected in user reported rates of "enjoyment, arousal, presence, immersion, and realism" (Kim and Sundar 2016, 45). Relatedly, screen and image size affect the extent to which people experience high levels of immersion or transportation (Grabe et al. 1999; Rigby et al. 2016; Sundar et al. 2017).

Accordingly, in line with our experimental results in Chapter 5, we expect (as reflected in H4, Table 2.2) information displays on smaller screens to induce lower rates of attentiveness and arousal as captured by HRV and SCL. More formally, we expect that *HRV will be lower when screen size is smaller*, and *SCL will decrease with screen size*.

CONTENT EFFECTS ON INFORMATION PROCESSING

Information processing is affected by the nature and tone of content, for example, political slant, emotional evocativeness and complexity, or negativity (Lang et al. 1995; Meffert et al. 2006). Among these possibilities, the latter is amongst the most well-investigated drivers of attentiveness and arousal. Negativity bias refers to the human tendency to prioritize negative information over positive or neutral information (Baumeister et al. 2001). This bias has been demonstrated across several fields and subfields across both physical and social sciences (Soroka 2014). In studies of information processing, evidence suggests that humans devote more cognitive effort to processing negative stimuli and, as a result, negativity causes us to focus our attention and pay more careful attention to details (Fiske 1980). In the real world, this plays out in people's preference for negative news stories over positive stories (Trussler and Soroka 2014). And there is a growing body of evidence for negativity biases using neurological and physiological measures as well. Brain activity is more apparent among lab subjects when shown pictures depicting unpleasant images, and exposure to negative information raises heart rate, blood pressure, and sweat excretion among lab subjects (Smith et al. 2003; Soroka and McAdams 2015).

Do these results vary alongside changes in structural constraints on information processing, such as screen size? We think they do. As H4 posits, smaller screens should lead to decreasing attentiveness and information processing generally; and this may be reflected in more limited reactions to attention-grabbing or thought-provoking information. To be clear: (a) physiological activation increases with negativity, and (b) attentiveness and information processing is more limited on smaller screens, so (c) we expect to find more limited variation in psychophysiological activation to negative versus positive stimuli on smaller screens. Reduced variation in activation in response to the tone of news content is thus used here as a way of exploring the constraining impact that screen size has on information processing.[3]

Mobile News Video Experiments

We test H4 using a lab experiment that examines the effects of mobile devices on attention to online news videos using psychophysiological measures, taking a similar approach to an experiment fielded by Soroka and McAdams (2015). Chapter 4 provides additional methodological information and an overview of our experimental approach (see Figure 4.1). We recruited a total of 113 participants from a university in the Midwest and in the South. Our sample was mostly female, and on average 19.6 years old (for sample details see Table A4.1). Participants were randomly assigned to watch a series of news stories on either a large- or small-screen, after which they then completed a survey online in the same lab. Thus, unlike our previous lab experiments, the manipulation most critical to this study is the random assignment of participants to either large- or small-screen conditions.[4] Screen size is thus a between-subjects factor, while story tone (negative and positive) is a within-subjects factor.[5] We manipulate screen size while holding all else constant to ensure we accurately estimate the impact of screen size on reactions to news stories. As the difference between the large- and small-screen treatments is not substantial, our tests are conservative (see Chapter 4 for more details).

As discussed in detail in Chapter 4, we rely on psychophysiological indicators of activation and engagement to capture the extent to which arousal, or attentiveness, varies systematically with video tone. To this end we measure SCL using the mean of "normalized" SCL across all seven stories with higher normalized SCL is taken to indicate greater levels of arousal. To expand our test of H4, we also explore a measure that captures variation in SCL across positive and negative video. We also measure HRV, two ways: (1) the standard deviation of the NN intervals (SDNN), calculated over each news story, and (2) the Root Mean Square of the Successive Differences (RMSSD); that is, the square root of the mean squared differences of successive NN intervals. We calculate both across all seven stories, excluding the inter-stimulus intervals.

We capture the impact of tone by estimating a simple time-series model for each participant, where "normalized" SCL for every one-second interval is regressed on (a) the overall tone of the video (Table A6.1), (b) a variable counting one-second intervals, and (c) a variable counting the number of videos (from one to seven). We further interact (a) and (b), which means that our model captures the impact of negativity, controlling for time in several ways, including the tendency for the impact of tone to dissipate over the course of a news video (as found in Soroka and McAdams 2015). We run this model for each participant, saving the coefficient for *Negativity*, which we conceptualize as an individual-level measure of the tendency to react more strongly to negative than to positive news content.

Results from the experiment are relatively straightforward. Regression models are presented in the Appendix (Table A6.1), with predicted values for psychophysiological measures across large- and small-screen treatments illustrated in Figure 6.1. The effects of screen size of both SDNN and RMSSD are illustrated in the first and second panels of Figure 6.1. That results are similar for both measures is an important indicator of robustness, confirming that our results are not dependent on one or the other measure of HRV. In line with H4, HRV decreases with screen size, and this is evident even when the screen manipulation is relatively small—from a laptop to mobile screen size.

The third panel of Figure 6.1 shows results from regressing overall SCL on screen size. The coefficient is in the expected direction (negative), but far from statistically significant. A significant constant indicates that arousal tends to be higher during news content then in the inter-stimulus periods, but the results do not suggest that screen size decreases stimulus-period arousal. We thus find no support for our expectation that SCL decreases with screen size.

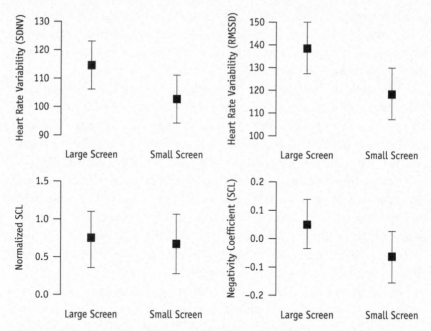

Figure 6.1 Predicted HRV and SCL with 95 percent confidence intervals, by screen size (Study 4) Notes: Predicted values correspond to models presented in Table A6.1 of the Appendix.

The final model (predicted values are illustrated in the rightmost panel of Figure 6.1) regresses our measure of reactivity to negative versus positive content on screen size. Here, we find marginally significant results in the expected direction. Note that we are using estimated regression coefficients as an independent variable here, and that there is a good deal of noise both in the models that produce this variable, and in the 102-respondent model in Table A6.1. We thus take even weak significance as an important signal.[6] Even as overall SCL does not decrease with screen size, then, the connection between SCL and the tone of video does. We take this as a sign that, in line with H4 and our general argument, the intensity of attentiveness and arousal in response to negative versus positive content increases with screen size. Alongside results for HRV, these results lend additional support to our argument that larger screens facilitate greater cognitive access to news content.

Conclusion

Drawing on our model of post-exposure processing, this chapter tests whether cognitive access to video news content—measured here using psychophysiological indicators of attentiveness and arousal—is reduced as viewers move to smaller screens. If attention is reduced on mobile devices, what is it about mobile devices that reduce attentiveness? In this chapter we lend additional confidence to results in Chapter 5 by isolating the effect of screen size. Here we also demonstrate replicability and robustness by using different physiological measures of interest and attention, varying the level of interestingness in the content, and by switching to video news content (Daignault, Soroka, and Giasson 2013; Soroka 2014; Soroka et al. 2016). Each participant viewed several news stories which varied by tone and interestingness. We found that small screens tend to decrease arousal over the course of the experiment, particularly for more interesting/negative news content. These findings demonstrate a potentially worrisome effect for cultivating informed mobile citizens: interest in news diminishes on smaller screens over the course of exposure to the story. This is true even among the most interesting news stories delivered in more engaging and less taxing video format.

Whether stories on mobile screens are less memorable or mobilizing cannot be assessed here. But past work suggests that physiological arousal is positively related to recall of video stimuli (Lang et al. 1995), that variance in physiological arousal is connected to differences in political knowledge (Grabe and Kamhawi 2006; Soroka et al. 2016), and that reactivity to information is associated with political participation (Gruszczynski et al. 2013). All this work points to the potential significance of our findings for political behavior, above and beyond the real-time reactions examined here. In Chapter 7 we put our hypotheses about the association between cognitive access and recall to the test.

7

Learning on Mobile Devices

The news media are the primary source through which citizens acquire political knowledge (Baum 2002, 2003; de Vreese and Boomgaarden 2006). This has not changed, but the way people access political news and information has changed dramatically (Dimmick, Feaster, and Hoplamazian 2011). Despite these dramatic shifts in the way people consume media, not since Prior (2007) and Bennett and Iyengar (2008), have we thoroughly revisited our major theories on the implications of the changing information landscape for media effects, especially as they pertain to political learning.

In Chapters 1 and 2 we laid out our argument for studying the impact of technological change on media effects as a product of how it shapes both pre-exposure (i.e., through technological effects on physical access to information, or the opportunity for exposure) and post-exposure processes (i.e., through technological effects on cognitive access to information and processing). Our view is supported by overlapping literature on the costs of pro-civic behaviors and information processing. Turning our empirical focus to post-exposure effects on cognitive access, in Chapters 5 and 6 we found that people pay less attention to news on mobile devices, suggesting potentially important consequences for what people know about politics.

In this chapter, we shift our focus to mobile effects on political learning. We look specifically at how news consumption on mobile devices affects information recall and uncover differential learning effects on mobile devices and computers. We also provide a test of whether the reduced attention we identified in earlier chapters is a byproduct of the cognitive effort required to access information on mobile devices. Further, we test whether this cognitive tax due to mobile access limits learning. In so doing, we test our proposed mechanism for why mobile constrains attention and the final portion of our model.

News and Democratic Citizens in the Mobile Era. Johanna Dunaway and Kathleen Searles, Oxford University Press. © Oxford University Press 2023. DOI: 10.1093/oso/9780190922504.003.0007

Changing Communication Technologies and Learning from News

Previous work examining information effects in an online environment typically focused on comparing media platforms (i.e., print, broadcast, and online). This work most often compared the impact of radio, television, newspapers, and magazines on content recall (Conway and Patterson 2008), and due to conflicting results, yielded little consensus. Some studies found that newspaper readers were better at recalling information than television viewers (Graber 1984; Bennett, Swenson, and Wilkinson 1992) while others found that television helped viewers recall information better (Katz, Adoni, and Parness 1977; Tichenor, Donohue, and Olien 1970). Researchers also found that recall was affected by reader sociodemographic factors, such as education and income; medium characteristics, such as visual and audio formats; contextual factors, such as the level of distraction among news watchers; and content characteristics, such as the importance attached to a story, proximity and incivility (Mutz 2015), and the quality of news programs (see Pipps et al. 2009 for a summary).

Research examining information recall in an online environment finds a similar impact of sociodemographic and medium-related factors. In one of the earliest studies examining the effect of online and print newspapers on readers' ability to recall information, Tewksbury and Althaus (2000) compared the readers of the print and online edition of the *New York Times* and found that compared to the print version, the online site provided fewer cues about a story's importance, such as story placement, story length, and headline size, but offered readers greater freedom to choose the stories they prefer to read. As a result, Tewksbury and Althaus (2000) concluded that readers were less likely to read or remember the front-page stories of the day, as compared to readers of print newspapers.

Similar to previous research comparing types of media platforms, d'Haenens et al.'s (2003) study revealed that the time spent reading the online and print version of a paper varied by gender, news topic, number of stories in each section, general knowledge, and level of interest. However, the overall impact of the two types of media on information recall was too mixed for the authors to come to a definite conclusion. In another study comparing different media, Conway and Patterson (2008) compared television and web recall and found that television viewers were better able to recall stories than web users, although the latter group remembered a broader variety of stories. The authors attributed this to differences in format. Print and television media present news in a linear, chronological order while online platforms present news in a non-linear, hyperlinked manner. While the format of presentation on print and television enables audiences to remember facts (Eveland, Seo, and Marton 2002), the online format encourages selective scanning and causes a decrease in factual learning (Eveland and Dunwoody 2002). Research also demonstrates how media can differentially affect perceptions of proximity, threat, and arousal—with consequences for memory and recall (Mutz 2015).

These documented differences in recall across various media platforms, and the fact that people consume news differently on various devices, echo our theory. We argue that the unique features of mobile devices make it more difficult to consume information, taxing available cognitive resources. These cognitive costs drain working memory bandwidth and the result is less executive control over attention and, ultimately, subpar learning outcomes. In short, information is harder to consume on smartphones and with fewer cognitive resources, users are less likely to pay attention, experience high rates of physiological arousal, or learn.

This hypothesized negative relationship between mobile device use and learning raises serious questions about the shift to mobile in a democracy. At the very least, it suggests the need for more scholarly attention on the sort of informational deficits we might expect as more people rely on their phones and tablets for news and politics. Still, research does not speak to the ways in which device use structures learning. Work on mobile technology focuses on learning outcomes within devices or on increased access to smartphones, while work on media effects focuses on the affordances provided by choice. Next, we offer some theoretical expectations.

Recall and Learning on Mobile Devices

Existing research on learning shows technological effects on information presentation, delivery, and structure have implications for learning and recall. In previous chapters we recounted the reasons this may be true; there is also existing work that explicitly deals with learning from information displayed on smaller screens. This work, too, supports our theory.

In this chapter we test two hypotheses. The first tests the theoretical mechanism posed in our model: cognitive effort. According to our theory, *consuming information is a costly endeavor and structural effects from the features of mobile devices increase those costs because they impede information processing.* We expect that paying attention to news on mobile devices requires more cognitive effort relative to computers. Specifically, our third hypothesis (see Table 2.2, H3) posits that *computer users will exhibit lower levels of cognitive effort relative to mobile device users.*

This cognitive drain explains why mobile users spend less time reading news than computers users, as we show in Chapter 5. As a result, this increased cognitive effort experienced by mobile device users translates to diminished attention and ultimately to poorer learning outcomes. We test this argument using our fifth hypothesis (see Table 2.2, H5), which posits that *the rate of recall should be higher among computer users relative to mobile users.* We test these hypotheses with two lab experiments and a quasi-experiment. The lab experiments permit us to test the mechanism: cognitive effort. Fortunately, eye-tracking methodology provides the means by which we can simultaneously observe the amount of visual attention paid to specific pieces of information and the cognitive effort being exerted to process the information (see Chapter 4 for more methodological details). The quasi-experiment uses an adult sample from an online labor market and allows participants to select the device they use and the content they prefer. As in previous chapters, mobile users include users of both tablets and smartphones. In this context we use recall to indicate learning given the link between diminished cognitive capacity and memory encoding. If, as we expect, processing information on mobile devices requires more cognitive effort, then this should negatively affect memory encoding.

As an overview, Study 1 provides the initial test of our hypotheses, Study 2 retests these hypotheses using a second lab experiment, and Study 3 replicates the testing of these hypotheses using a non-student sample, shoring up external validity via a participant preference design. We discuss the lab experiment details and results first, following up this discussion with Study 3 (see Figure 4.1 for a visual of our empirical approach).

Mobile Learning Lab Experiments

In this chapter we test H3 and H5. We review some key methodological details here but interested readers should also read Chapter 4. Both studies are pre-post lab experiments and feature student samples. A total of 171 students were recruited to participate in two lab studies and randomly assigned to read a news article on either a smartphone, tablet, or computer. Our sample was, on average, twenty years old, white, Republican, and female (for sample details see Table A4.1). The use of students is not only convenient, but also offers us the opportunity to study the effects of mobile devices on a population that is savvy with such technology. Upon arrival to the lab, participants first complete a pre-test questionnaire measuring demographics. Afterwards, they are asked to read a news story stimulus on their assigned device. In the post-test questionnaire, participants are then asked open- and close-ended questions about the news story they read. The appearance and format of the news article was the same for each group; see Figure 4.2 and 4.3 for stimuli. Recall that Study 1 features three groups assigned to read on a smartphone, tablet, or computer, while Study 2 includes the last two conditions only to maximize statistical power.

Similar to Chapter 5, we used eye trackers to capture physiological data to test our hypotheses. For the *Computer* condition we employ a desktop with an internal eye tracker. For the *Tablet* and *Smartphone* conditions we employ an external tracker setup; see Figure 4.5. Eye trackers capture two outcomes of interest for this chapter—the amount of time people spent fixated on news content, or *Reading Time*, and differences in pupillary response (pupil size), or *Cognitive Effort* (Wang, Spezio, and Camerer 2010, 1; Wang 2011). The first, *Reading Time*, is captured unobtrusively by the eye tracker and measured as the total seconds participants spent fixating on the body of the article, an indicator of top-down processing. This is the same measure used to capture attention in Chapter 5.

The second outcome, *Cognitive Effort*, indicates logged averaged pupil size (left and right) for each fixation to the body of the story, providing a continuous measure of cognitive demands during exposure. Thus, *Cognitive Effort* allows us to operationalize the psycho-physiological costs of information-seeking by point of access and test H3. The eye tracker offers an obvious advantage over asking people to report the cognitive demands of a task. Decades of research demonstrate the efficacy of pupillometry in the examination of cognitive processes (Beatty and Lucero-Wagoner 2000) and pupillary response has been found to consistently predict task complexity across a variety of stimuli (Beatty 1982). Simply, when engaging in a difficult task, such as reading a news article, pupils are known to dilate in response to the cognitive demand (Beatty 1982; Chatham, Frank, and Munakata 2009). Fortunately, eye trackers offer a method for measuring pupil size changes.

A third outcome, *Recall*, indicates the total number of correct answers participants give to three post-test questions testing their comprehension level (Study 1) or the number of details participants offer in a posttest open-ended question (Study 2; see Table A4.2 for measure details by study). Because we want to know not just how many details people recall, but how many details they recall given time spent reading the news article, where appropriate (and given no violation of the equal dispersion assumption) we estimate a Poisson model with duration of device exposure as an offset. An offset variable is a covariate with its coefficient set to one. Offsets are useful here for theoretical and methodological reasons. First, recall our model anticipates differential rates of recall due to known differences in behavior across computers and mobile devices. This approach allows us to model varying lengths of exposure rather than assuming constant exposure. Second, methodologically, using an offset is similar to, but more efficient than, including duration of exposure as a predictor. Ultimately, using this modeling strategy we can estimate the difference in expected log rates (*Recall/Reading Time*), and test H5.

In Study 2 we additionally capture *Recall 24-Hours Later*, operationalized the same way as *Recall*, just collected via survey twenty-four hours after exposure. This additional measure permits a test of the effects of device on recall both immediately after the experiment *and* a day later.

Note that as differences in log rates make little intuitive sense, we use an equation to derive expected counts, which tells us the expected number of items correctly recalled per average time on device.

The formula is as follows:

$$\ln\left(\frac{Recall}{Reading\ Time}\right) = \beta_0 + \beta_1\left(Tablet\right) + \beta_2\left(Smartphone\right)$$

Because $ln\left(\dfrac{a}{b}\right) = \ln(a) - \ln(b)$, we can rewrite this model with $\ln(Reading\ Time)$ as an offset variable:

$$ln(Recall) = \beta_0 + \beta_1\left(Tablet\right) + \beta_2\left(Smartphone\right) + ln\left(Reading\ Time\right).$$

In Study 1 we model these outcomes as a function of two predictors for *Smartphone* and *Tablet*, dummy variables where the comparison category is computer user. In Study 2 we follow the same approach with one predictor for *Tablet*. The full tables for each model can be found in the Appendix. The results are robust to alternative model specifications, including the use of a right-censored Poisson model for Study 1.

The first set of results are shown in Figure 7.1. Recall H3 suggests that features of tablets and smartphones require users to draw on more cognitive resources relative to computer users and, as a result, consuming information on these mobile devices requires more cognitive effort. *Cognitive Effort* is indicated by more dilated pupils. As we can see in the figure, pupil size for tablet and smartphone users is significantly larger than computer users, offering support for H3. These results persist whether we average across pupils or look at a single pupil at a time.

Next we test H5. We expect that these higher cognitive costs paired with diminished attention (as we show in Chapter 5) will lead tablet and smartphone users to recall fewer items than computer users. To test H5, we deploy a Poisson regression model with an offset, which allows us to estimate rates of recall that vary by *Reading Time*. While both the *Tablet* and *Smartphone* coefficients are

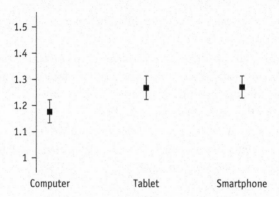

Figure 7.1 Predicted cognitive effort with 95 percent confidence intervals, by device (Study 1) Notes: Predictions are from model presented in Table A7.1 in the Appendix. The outcome variable, *Cognitive Effort*, is the logged averaged pupil size (left and right). The comparison group for device is computer.

significant (see Table A7.2), we calculate the expected number of facts recalled by treatment group using the formula above for ease of interpretation. Recall first that the average reading time is 52.31 seconds for computer users, 12.20 second for tablet users, and 18.49 seconds for smartphone users. As a result, computer users are found to have the largest count of correct factual recall (2.48), followed by tablet (2.39), and then smartphone users (2.31). The differences are statistically significant yet small, suggesting that people reading the news article on a tablet or smartphone recalled fewer facts about the story than people reading the news article on a computer, given duration of exposure.

To lend more meaning to these small differences, we can examine the rate, or number of facts people recalled per condition: computer users are found to have the smallest rate of facts recalled (.05), followed by tablet (.18), and then smartphone users (.13). How then, can computer uses recall more facts overall but have a poorer *rate* of recall? A closer look at the data reveals that computer users recall more *because they spend more time reading*. Indeed, if we were to interpret the model without reading time, then we may walk away thinking mobile users outperformed computer users. While there is more variability among mobile device users, with mobile users that spend longer on the task performing better, computer users consistently spend longer times reading and thus, recall more facts. Considered alongside the significant rates of *Cognitive Effort* among mobile users, the evidence suggests that, on balance, mobile device users expend more cognitive effort, and spend less time reading, and the result is less learning relative to computer users.

In Study 2, we focus only on the *Tablet* and *Computer* conditions and we took the additional step of following-up with participants twenty-four hours after

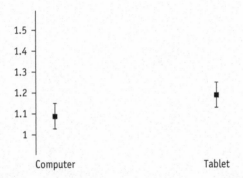

Figure 7.2 Predicted cognitive effort with 95 percent confidence intervals, by device (Study 2) Notes: Predictions are from model presented in Table A7.3 in the Appendix. The outcome variable, *Cognitive Effort*, is the logged averaged pupil size (left and right). The comparison group for device is computer.

exposure to ask them once more to list all the details they remembered from the news article. Otherwise, in Study 2 we take the same steps as Study 1, estimating the effects of *Tablet* and *Computer* on *Recall, Recall 24-hours Later,* and *Cognitive Effort.*

To test H3 we examine the effects of device on *Cognitive Effort*; the results are displayed in Figure 7.2. Like Study 1, the pupil size for tablet users is significantly larger than computer users. These results lend additional support to H3 and suggest that tablet users encounter greater cognitive demands when consuming information.

We also again examine *Recall* by device as a second test of H5. The average reading time is 66.59 seconds for computer users, and 66.09 second for tablet users. Using the same approach as Study 1, the model yields an insignificant coefficient for *Tablet*, suggesting that, for Study 2, the rate of *Recall* does not significantly differ between tablet and computer users (see Table A7.4). However, the expected number of correct facts recalled by device is in the expected direction, with computer users recalling more (4.32) than tablet users (4.07). When we look at the expected number of facts recalled by condition twenty-four hours later, we see a familiar pattern revealing more significant differences between conditions: computer users recalled the most details (3.92), followed by tablet users (2.48); displayed in Figure 7.3 with standard errors.

Altogether Study 2 replicates the *Cognitive Effort* results from Study 1 and provides mixed evidence for our *Recall* results. Consistently across studies, we see mobile users exert more cognitive effort. They are also, as a result, learning less (Study 1) and recalling less a day later (Study 2), given average duration of exposure. As a robustness check, we conduct a third study on a more representative sample using an online labor market. We discuss this study next.

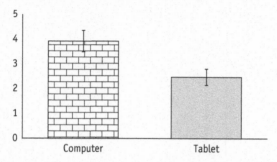

Figure 7.3 Predicted count of recall 24 hours later, by device (Study 2) Notes: Predictions are from model presented in Table A7.5 in the Appendix. The outcome variable, *Recall*, ranges from 0 to 8 based on the number of facts reported in open-ended post-test prompts. The comparison group for device is computer.

Does Reading News on Mobile Devices Affect Learning? A Non-student Replication

We designed our third study as a quasi-experiment to supplement the two lab studies previously presented, drawing participants from an online labor market. By triangulating multiple methods to test our hypotheses, we can overcome two methodological barriers that plague media effects research: the unreliability of self-report media consumption, and the lack of mundane realism in forced exposure designs. The two lab studies improve upon self-report by using data collected outside of participant awareness via eye trackers. This is coupled with superior internal validity via experimental control and random assignment of treatments. Yet as with most lab experiments, it lacks external validity because it does not reflect media consumption in a real-world setting. Studies of media effects are often criticized for low levels of external validity, such as a failure to allow for media choice.

In Study 3 we privilege mundane realism in the effort to improve upon gener-alizability. The online labor market sample offers an improvement upon the arti-ficiality of the lab because participants can consume the media stimuli and take the survey in an environment of their choosing. Moreover, given the increased statistical power, we also permit people to select the stimulus they would prefer to read, whether a news article or entertainment article. Given the importance of media choice in today's media environment, this design allows us to better understand media consumption behaviors, which are often guided by audience convenience (Arceneaux and Johnson 2013). In addition, and perhaps most importantly, this sample affords participants their choice of device on which they execute the study. People inclined to complete studies on their phones or tablets self-selected into the mobile device condition. It is reasonable to believe that participants who use their mobile device to complete a study are also likely to use the same device to consume information.[1] Because the survey is delivered online we are not able to collect pupil dilation data, so for this study we focus on H5.

These design choices left us with a 2 x 3 non-equivalent groups design ($N = 857$), with media choice (news vs. entertainment) and device choice (computer, tablet, smartphone). Participants were recruited through an online labor market, Amazon's Mechanical Turk; more details on this study are provided in the Appendix. Upon providing informed consent, participants first completed a pre-test questionnaire measuring political orientation, habitual media use, and general media trust; afterwards, they were asked to select the news or entertainment story they preferred to read (see Figure 4.4). The presentation order of the two stories was randomized. In the post-test questionnaire, participants were then asked open- and close-ended questions about the story they read and questions aimed at discerning who took the study using a mobile device. Participants self-selected into device condition with their choice of device to complete the study: a computer, tablet, or smartphone. Instead of asking respondents to self-report the device they used, we asked them to identify the device with the following instructions: "This study includes reading news articles with pictures. Please make sure that you are able to see pictures before continuing. Below are three pictures of the previous instruction page you've just read, please choose one that looks mostly similar to the one shown on your screen." The images presented to participants were manipulated so as to approximate screenshots of the mobile Qualtrics interface versus the computer Qualtrics interface. To maximize the number of observations in mobile device conditions, responses to this question were recoded into a dummy variable with 1 representing mobile use (smartphone and tablet) and 0 representing computer use (laptops and desktops). We also took additional precautions to ensure an accurate accounting of the device used. See Table A4.6 and proximate discussion in the Appendix for details.

Similar to lab Studies 1 and 2, to test H5 we measure *Recall*, which indicates the total number of correct answers participants give to several questions, taking into account *Reading Time*. *Reading Time* is captured automatically by Qualtrics and measured as the total seconds participants spent on the page. Although this operationalization of *Reading Time* lacks the nuance of our lab studies, which capture actual visual attention using eye tracking, it provides a rough approximation which permits a meaningful comparison. We model *Recall* as a function of a predictor for *Mobile*, a dummy variable that captures smartphone or tablet use where the comparison category is computer user. Because most participants opted to take the survey on a computer (N = 733, 85.5 percent) compared to tablet and smartphone users (N = 124, 14.5 percent), we pool tablet and smartphone users into one condition for mobile device.

Recall that H5 predicts that mobile users will remember fewer items than people reading on their computers. To test this, we regress the *Mobile* indicator on the *Recall* variable. We again include *Reading Time* as an offset, which permits us to model rates given people's varying amount of exposure to the stimulus (see Table A7.6 for full model). A significant coefficient for *Mobile* indicates differences between the two groups. Akin to Study 1 and 2, we calculate the expected number of facts recalled by group for ease of interpretation and generate the expected number of count of facts recalled across the mobile and computer groups, taking into account their varied exposure time. Computer users have the largest count of correct factual recall. The predicted count of correct recalls is 2.5 for computer users who spent an average of 100.39 seconds reading the article; on the other hand, mobile users who spent an average of 81.11 seconds reading news have predicted recall of 2.40. Again, the differences are small, but considered alongside the results presented from the two lab experiments above, there is compelling evidence that consuming information on tablets and smartphones results in less learning, relative to computer users.

Conclusion

We are situated in a time during which the mobile age meets the fragmented media environment. As a result, people can read any news outlet, anywhere, given access to a tablet or smartphone. While the proliferation of cable and the internet gives some reasons for optimism, we find that mobile devices pose limitations for learning. We argue that the features of mobile devices exert cognitive costs, and that this cost structures attention in a way that results in unequal information acquisition between mobile and computer users. Our theory informs two hypotheses—H3 and H5—which we test using two lab experiments featuring eye-tracking technology, and replicate using a third quasi-experiment using an adult sample.

In H3, we hypothesize that information acquisition on mobile devices requires more cognitive effort relative to computers. Using pupil dilation, a measure of cognitive effort, captured via eye trackers in two lab experiments, we find that people consuming information on mobile devices endure a higher cognitive burden than computer users. As cost is the mechanism underlying our model, these results support our general orientation towards portraying information consumption as a costly endeavor made more so in the mobile environment.

Because of these increased cognitive demands, we expect that diminished cognitive resources result in poorer learning outcomes upon exposure to information on a mobile device, as articulated in H5. We find support for this hypothesis in Study 1 and 3, and when measured twenty-four hours later in Study 2, buoying our theoretical framework. Overall, these results suggest mobile devices influences readers' ability to recall information from news stories.

These results highlight challenges for the information consumption and learning in a mobile environment. Building on a wealth of work in multiple disciplines, from communication to computer-mediated communication to political science, we argue that information consumption is costly and that mobile devices pose additional challenges that negatively affect learning. In previous chapters, we also demonstrate that attention is relatively fleeting on mobile devices. As a consequence, these costs associated with the mobile information environments attenuate people's attention to information, and this affects their ability to recall that information.

In the second lab experiment we ask users again twenty-four hours later what they remember from what they read, and we find that computer users recall advantage over mobile users grows greatly. And while the magnitude of effects we found are not large, given increasing international migration to mobile devices from computers, even small changes towards less recall to information on mobile devices is likely to have consequences over time. Moreover, we asked participants to recall only the most basic facts after reading the news article—given a more complex task, such as looking up a member of Congress or filtering various viewpoints on a given policy, we imagine the effects to be more dramatic. On the other hand, when people perform less complex tasks—like scrolling through a social media feed or texting a friend—we may see insignificant differences in terms of learning and cognitive costs. It seems likely that mobile costs are task-dependent, and such questions deserve more scholarly attention. However, it is no less concerning or of import that a task like we present here, reading an article on a device, results in suboptimal learning. Moreover, these tests are conservative: our participants are young, mobile-adept students, likely susceptible to demand effects in an unnatural lab environment, and yet still, when assigned to a mobile device they spend less time reading the story, draw down more cognitive resources, recall fewer details, and this disadvantage persists as time wears on. We expect that these effects are even more dramatic among non-college samples.

8

Putting Traffic to the Test

Mobile News Attention in the Wild

The results from our lab experiments in Chapter 5 and 6 suggest that mobile devices limit attention to and emotional engagement with news content. When people spend less time focused on news stories, as we show in Chapter 7, the consequence is diminished learning from the stories they read. While there are methodological benefits to our approach (detailed in Chapter 4), it is reasonable to wonder whether these results generalize to the real world, where news outlets are actually competing for the attention of the digital news audience.

We set out to answer this question by revisiting the Comscore dataset we first analyzed in Chapter 3, with an eye toward bolstering the external validity of our mobile attention experiments with real-world web traffic data. While this data has been historically hard to come by, a big picture look at web traffic patterns by point of access is essential to understanding how communication technology shapes news consumption on the internet (Hindman 2009). Web traffic data gives scale to information consumption on the internet, only a very small portion of which goes to news sites, despite limited scholarly attention to such limited exposure. Much like Hindman (2009) uses web link density data to demonstrate the ways political information is constrained by the choice architecture of the web, we use web traffic data to demonstrate that people spend more time on news sites when they are on computers than when they are on tablets and smartphones. Important nuances among different types of mobile news consumers are also revealed. News app users—ostensibly more interested in news—spend more time on news than those who arrive to news sites through mobile browsers, yet their proportion of the mobile news audience is a mere fragment relative to those reaching news websites via browsers.

News and Democratic Citizens in the Mobile Era. Johanna Dunaway and Kathleen Searles, Oxford University Press. © Oxford University Press 2023. DOI: 10.1093/oso/9780190922504.003.0008

Consistent with what we showed in the lab, these real-world results underscore the ways mobile news consumption is limited by cognitive access. These data also enable us to better navigate the two conflicting accounts of mobile internet access posed in Chapter 1; specifically, whether internet proliferation on mobile devices is the great digital leveler or instead, the impetus for second class digital citizenship (Mossberger, Tolbert, and Franko 2013). Although not a silver bullet, our data suggest reasons for both optimism and skepticism; even as most users spend little time consuming news on their smartphones, a small few spend a *lot* of time on news apps.

Testing Mobile News Attention in the Wild

As we note in Chapter 3, Comscore leases a proprietary dataset for academic use—they include web traffic data for most major national news outlets, across devices (computers, tablets, smartphones) based on one-quarter of a million users.[1] It offers an unparalleled look at real world news consumption. In this chapter, we examine whether there are differences in the amount of time individual visitors spend on sites by mode of access. We focus on two media-industry measures designed to capture levels of news attention and engagement: site minutes per visitor and site minutes per visit. The web traffic data we analyze are from March 2016.

DATA

The Comscore data provide per visitor and per visit data on audience traffic to news and entertainment websites, broken down by smartphones, tablets, and computers, as well as by browser and app-based access. Because they are based on actual audience traffic to news sites, the Comscore data allow for a validity check on our lab studies.

Digital news outlets comprise the unit of *analysis*, while the units of *observation* are points of access to each outlets' content ($N = 1,052$), which is based on measures of outlets' site traffic from visitors using computers, tablets, and smartphones. Each outlet can have traffic from three to five different possible points of access. For example, there are five observations, or points of access, associated with cnn.com: cnn.com-computer-browser, cnn.com-tablet-browser, cnn.com-tablet-app, cnn.com-smartphone-browser, and cnn.com smartphone-app. The points of access are nested within outlets, mandating that we cluster our standard errors at the news outlet level.[2] Here we use these data to model time spent on news sites per visit as a function of mode of access (i.e., computers, tablets, and smartphones).

MEASURES

We use two outcome variables to capture attention duration with the Comscore data. First, *Average Minutes per Visitor*, measures the average number of minutes spent on the news site during the month of March 2016, per individual visitor (Comscore 2016). Second, *Average Minutes per Visit*, indicates the average number of minutes spent on the news site per visit for the same time period. Due to the skewness of each, we use logged values. Similar to our measurement approach in Chapter 5, we model these outcomes as a function of two main predictors, dichotomous indicators for *Tablet* or *Smartphone*, with *Computer* serving as the baseline. In the models predicting *Average Minutes per Visitor*, we also include a variable for *App*, which captures site access sites via news app (coded as 1) or web browser (coded as 0). See Appendix for summary information.[3]

RESULTS

Table A8.1 (see Appendix for this chapter) presents an identity-gamma generalized model and two OLS regression models. Two predict average minutes per visitor spent on sites, one predicts average minutes spent on sites per visit. The first column presents the full model on minutes per visitor controlling for app versus browser access; the second model is for browser users only.[4] Again, we see a significant and negative coefficient for *Tablet* and *Smartphone*, supporting our first hypothesis regarding attention duration: relative to computer users, tablet and smartphone users spend significantly less time on news sites on a per visitor basis, which is consistent across specifications. Interestingly, the results from the full model suggest that, even when controlling for app access, users spend less time attending to news on tablets or smartphones. While the number of app users is too small to estimate a full model, the descriptive data reveal that smartphone app users spend an average of 7.56 minutes on news sites compared to 2.15 minutes via browser.

The third model in Table A8.1 displays the results from a regression model predicting average minutes per site visit, which provide partial support for H1 (also see Figure 8.2). A significant and negative coefficient for *Smartphone* indicates users spend significantly less time on news sites, relative to computer users. The indicator for *Tablet* is not statistically significant.

The predicted values for average minutes per visitor with ninety-five percent confidence intervals are displayed in Figure 8.1. The figure shows that tablet and smartphone visitors to news sites spend significantly *less* time on the sites relative to computer users.[5] Perhaps most troublesome, given our earlier analysis of audience reach and physical access to information, is that when we look at the amount of time people spend on sites by device, we find more evidence for the

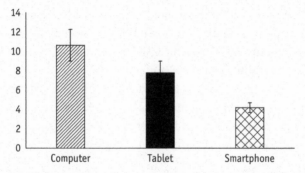

Figure 8.1 Predicted average minutes per visitor with 95 percent confidence intervals, by device (Study 5) Notes: Data are from Comscore, Media Metrix Data for March 2016. Predicted values correspond to Model 2 in Table A8.1 of the Appendix. The comparison group for tablets and smartphones is computers. Predictions are generated for users accessing news sites via browsers.

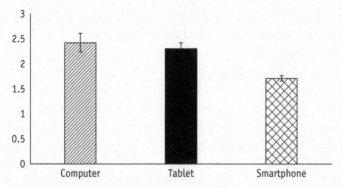

Figure 8.2 Predicted average minutes per visit with 95 percent confidence intervals, by device (Study 5) Notes: Data are from Comscore, Media Metrix Data for March 2016. Predicted values correspond to Model 3 in Table A8.1 of the Appendix. The comparison group for tablets and smartphones is computers. Predictions are generated for users accessing news sites via browsers.

breadth versus depth trade-off. Media content reaches many more people on smartphones relative to tablets and computers, but smartphone users spend substantially less time on news sites relative to tablet and computer users. Computer visitors, for example, spend more than twice the amount of time on news sites as their smartphone counterparts. The means by which most audiences are reached is the one that appears to limit attention and engagement the most.

It is possibly more instructive to examine the impact of device use on the amount of time people spend on sites per visit. This is a more direct measure of how engaged people are with the content each time they arrive to a site. Figure 8.2 shows the average minutes per visit to news by device. Here again we see the disconnect between audience reach and engagement. The general pattern of computer users spending more time on sites holds, and we again see a shorter duration per visit for smartphone users. When we examine engagement at the minutes per visit level, we see that—for those vast audiences accessing sites through their smartphones—the visits are substantially shorter in duration, indicating less engagement with site content.

These analyses support the results we report in Chapter 5: device matters for attention to news, and this relationship is consistent by manner of access. The Comscore data enable a real-world robustness check, illustrating web use patterns by device. Mobile devices constrain time spent on news sites on a per visit and per visitor basis.

Conclusion

In this chapter, we investigate whether mobile devices constrain news attention among real-world computer, tablet, and smartphone users. To do this we use computer and mobile web-traffic data from news websites. These data are industry quality measures of website performance based on actual visitor behaviors and lend additional support to our lab results on attention and engagement. The proprietary data, collected by Comscore, offer a glimpse into mobile consumption across a variety of news sites. Specifically, we use this website-level aggregate data from "the wild" to replicate the results from our experimental studies.

Drawing on measures of average minutes per site, and average minutes on site per visit, and browser- versus application-based visits, we demonstrate that, much like in the lab, time spent with online political news content on mobile devices is fleeting relative to computer users. Taken alongside our experimental studies, this aggregate web-tracking data presents an externally valid and conservative real world test of the arguments we advance.

9

News Exposure and Information Processing in a Post-Broadcast Media Environment

The arguments and evidence we present in this book offer empirical, theoretical, and methodological contributions. These contributions have important normative implications for how communication technologies can help or hinder an informed democratic citizenry, and they have practical implications, for journalists and news consumers in an increasingly digital, social, and mobile media environment. In this final chapter, we review these contributions, discuss the implications, and argue for the utility of our framework and theory for future research.

Empirical Contributions

A central tenant of our theoretical argument is that there are important distinctions in terms of how changing media technologies shape physical versus cognitive access to information. In Chapter 3, we begin by making a descriptive case for this argument. We demonstrate how the proliferation of mobile devices is expanding physical access to information—by expanding the digital media audience more generally—and how its impact is disproportionate across demographic groups, countries, and regions. We also show—using a few major U.S. news websites as exemplars—how despite the increasing reach of mobile devices, most mobile visits to news sites are fleeting. Even as the breadth of the audience is increasing, the depth of news encounters afforded by mobile (albeit more frequent) is reduced.

News and Democratic Citizens in the Mobile Era. Johanna Dunaway and Kathleen Searles, Oxford University Press. © Oxford University Press 2023. DOI: 10.1093/oso/9780190922504.003.0009

We conclude Chapter 3 with a robust set of tests using web traffic data from Comscore. The tests based on these data show the consequences mobile devices can have for breadth over depth: mobile represents a trade-off between physical and cognitive access to information. Much of the mobile digital news audience are smartphone users, but they are only minimally engaged with content. As a result, although many more people reach news sites through smartphones, these visits tend to be significantly shorter than visits via computers. Our theory of post-exposure processing (PEP) provides an explanation for this evidence.

In Chapter 5 we present findings from experimental studies designed to test hypotheses about whether mobile devices curb attention to news and links embedded in news stories. Looking to effects on attention, H2 posits a negative relationship between mobile device use and time spent reading news. We find support for this hypothesis in Study 1, where we find shorter duration of attention among both tablet and smartphone users relative to those on computers. When we examine the relationship between mobile device use and attention paid to news links, results show that mobile device users are less likely to notice news links at all, and when they do, they fixate on them for less time, relative to computer users. In Study 2, we replicate tests of news attention from Study 1, but using a more conservative test between only tablet and computer users. With the exception of time spent reading the news content, where we do not observe significant differences in duration of attention between tablet and computer users, the Study 1 results replicate. Overall, the data suggest that when people consume information on a tablet or smartphone, they are paying less attention to news.

Building on these studies of attention, in Chapter 6 we field psychophysiological experiments to test H4, which posits that mobile sized screens reduce attention *and* arousal. These studies differ from those presented in Chapter 5 in four important ways, where each difference in the design accomplishes one of two things: (1) to ensure that our main finding—that mobile devices limit attention—is not an artifact of news format, the use of eye tracking, story type, or tone; and (2) to isolate screen size as a primary mechanism for the effect. We do this by using online video news stories as stimuli, rather than text-based stories; isolating the effect of screen size by conducting the experiment entirely on laptops, varying only the dimensions of the window in which the video news story is shown; varying the tone of stories within-subjects, and relying on a different set of psychophysiological indicators for measurement of our key outcome variables. Cognitive access is defined operationally as either heart rate variability (HRV), capturing a combination of activation and engagement, or skin conductance level (SCL), which indicates activation or arousal. Using both

HRV and SCL, our findings suggest that screen size limits cognitive access to online video news, and even more so for negative online video news.

Having established attentional differences across a range of methods and outcomes, in Chapter 7 we turn to the mechanism and consequences of these differences. Our theory informs two hypotheses, H3 and H5. In H3, we hypothesize that information acquisition on mobile devices requires more cognitive effort relative to computers. Central to our theoretical arguments, this hypothesis tests the mechanism underlying the effects observed in Chapters 5 and 6: cognitive effort. Eye-tracking methodology—the measurement of pupil dilation in particular—provides the means by which we can simultaneously observe the amount of visual attention paid to specific pieces of information, and the cognitive effort being exerted to process the information. Using pupil dilation as a measure of cognitive effort, we find support for H3. Those consuming information on mobile devices endure a higher cognitive burden than those on computers. These results support our portrayal of information consumption as a costly endeavor, and these costs are magnified on mobile devices.

Because of these increased cognitive demands, we expect that diminished cognitive resources result in poorer learning outcomes upon exposure to information on a mobile device. Our fifth hypothesis, H5, posits that rates of recall of information from news stories should be higher among computer users relative to mobile users. We test this hypothesis with two lab experiments and a quasi-experiment. We find evidence in support of this hypothesis in Study 1 and Study 3, and when measured twenty-four hours later in Study 2. Overall, this chapter offers evidence of the cognitive demands and attentional limits imposed by mobile devices, and the resultant consequences for learning.

In Chapter 8, in an effort to investigate whether our lab findings would replicate in a real-world context, we retest H1 with Comscore data. We generate several models, predicting average minutes per visitor spent on sites and average minutes spent on sites per visit. The results from both support H1: relative to computer users, tablet and smartphone users spend significantly less time on news sites per visitor and per visit.

Overall, our web traffic analyses lend support to our lab-based experimental findings. Consistently we show that people spend more time on news sites when they are on computers relative to smartphones. These patterns are also true for tablet users, although the negative relationship between tablet and time does not reach traditional levels of significance. By and large, the data show that digital media content reaches many more people on mobile devices relative to computers, but smartphone users and tablet users spend less time on news sites. The means by which most digital audiences are reached is the one that appears to limit attention and engagement the most.

Methodological Contributions

The empirical and theoretical contributions offered in this book were made possible by our ability to draw on a toolbox of underused methods and measures, which are uniquely suited to capturing information processing and the cognitive effort it requires. While eye tracking and psychophysiological methods are gaining traction in both political science and communication research (Vraga et al. 2016; Vraga et al. 2019; Wagner et al. 2015; Soroka, Fournier, Nir, and Hibbing 2019; Soroka 2019; Settle et al. 2020), we hope our use of these methods will encourage more researchers studying media effects to consider how these tools might enhance or expand their work, potentially in ways that will make more substantial contributions to the broader research endeavor.

The long history of media effects reveals ongoing challenges with measuring both news exposure and its effects on attention and processing (e.g., Zaller 1992, 1996). Our psychophysiological work in this book makes a methodological contribution by illustrating how these tools provide one fruitful way to deal with the latter, and that they can also help elucidate the conditions under which exposure does and does not equate to attention. The media effects literature also highlights how challenges to measurement—especially with respect to news exposure and attention—have intermittently stalled the advancement of theory (e.g., Iyengar and Kinder 1987). We have argued that a failure to account for technological effects on post-exposure processing damages our ability to fully understand what the changing media environment means for media effects, and we hope, that by articulating a uniquely suited methodological approach, we offer one path forward.

In addition, we bolster these methodological contributions by triangulating across methods, measures, and samples wherever possible. It is too often the case that fragmented literatures in political communication are attributable to differences in methodological approaches (although this problem is not unique to political communication). Experimental studies of selective exposure to partisan news (e.g., Iyengar and Hahn 2009), for example, have frequently yielded evidence and conclusions in stark opposition to observational studies of the same phenomenon (e.g., Nelson and Webster 2017). By providing evidence and findings robust to the use of several different types of experiments, samples, data, and units and levels of observation, we hope this study serves as an exemplar.

LIMITATIONS

Along with the contributions they offer, our studies and methods have limitations. The primary limitation is that—despite our efforts to triangulate with observational data and non-lab experiments—our lab studies rely on small-n student samples. Although we acknowledge that for many the use of undergraduate student samples is a serious limitation, we suspect that our use of student samples provides a more conservative test of our hypotheses. The age cohort represented in our samples is more likely to have extensive experience with mobile devices; we expect that any differences we observe would be more pronounced rather than less so, among non-college age participants.

In defense of our approach we also offer what is likely an arguable point: the use of psychophysiological measures as outcome variables makes the use of student samples slightly less problematic.[1] This is certainly true from the standpoint of response bias. Our analyses rely on physiological quantities, not on self-reported data. This is because we do not expect participants—of any age or education level—to be able to accurately assess their attentiveness to news stories or information processing. While there are obvious trade-offs in the use of college samples we believe they are offset in this case by our ability to use physiological measures, which we regard as the best-possible indicators of real-time attention and information processing.

It is also the case that the time and technology required of both our eye-tracking studies and those using HRV and SCL necessitate smaller samples. The cost of the equipment required limits the number of properly equipped lab machines available, making it impossible to run more than a few subjects at a time. This is common to this kind of research; many psychophysiological studies are only equipped to run two subjects at a time (Settle et al. 2020). As such, it is not uncommon for such studies to be small-n. Additionally, eye-tracking studies require experimenters to calibrate the eye movements of each participant prior to delivering the test. Similarly, those running physiological studies must manually assist participants with attaching finger monitors to measure HRV and HCL. They must also carefully observe participants to ensure high-quality data collection, noting things such as disruption, or sudden or prolonged movement—anything that might interfere with accurate reading of the data. For all of these reasons, our sample of 113 in Study 4 is relatively large according to the standards for such studies; our N is more in line with recommended practices for reducing biased estimates in psychophysiological research. Baldwin (2017), for example, compares the precision of estimates from small n to studies of 50, 100, and 150 participants, and documents the precision is much higher, even for studies with an n of only 50. The samples for eye-tracking studies tend to range widely; our research and a few meta-analyses suggest the median N is somewhere around 80 participants, placing the sample size from our eye-tracking studies within reasonable bounds at 115 and 56 (İşbilir et al. 2019; Platt et al. 2021). For all the reasons outlined in Chapter 4, the benefits of using eye-tracking and psychophysiological measures significantly outweigh these limitations.

Theoretical Contributions

THE DEBATE ON MOBILE ACCESS

Until now, we did not know precisely how news attention and engagement on mobile devices differed relative to more traditional means of consumption, and we lacked a theoretical context capable of explaining who is affected and under what circumstances. Our book advances theories regarding the impact of mobile devices by blending insights from research spanning several fields, highlighting the barriers mobile devices present for news audiences. Specifically, we offer a framework that helps us understand current divides in perceptions about the impact of mobile devices on digital divides. Once we view expanding mobile access through the lens of physical and cognitive access (PCA), reasons behind disparate interpretations regarding mobile's democratizing potential become clear. Mobile communication technology is expanding physical access to information because it provides a more affordable and convenient manner of accessing the internet. Yet even as mobile expands physical access through its versatile and convenient features, those same features shape information in ways that curb cognitive access.

Additionally, we put forth the PEP theory, drawing on a psychologically informed rational choice model, generating an explanation for information processing challenges on mobile devices. We argue, and ultimately find, that news engagement and attention are curbed on mobile devices because of the many information seeking and cognitive costs their features impose.

We adopt this theoretical approach because it is important that we anticipate and explain the conditions under which mobile devices produce important information consequences. We reconcile views describing mobile internet access as the cause versus the solution to digital divides. Mobile is both of these things, although the direction of effects will depend heavily on informational, individual, and contextual characteristics. In order to understand what differential rates of access mean for various individuals and groups across contexts, it was necessary to first document and explain the important baseline differences in attention, engagement, and recall when exposure to news and political information occurs on mobile devices.

UNDERSTANDING MEDIA EFFECTS IN THE DIGITAL ERA

In addition to speaking to debates about the effects of mobile, we make a broader theoretical contribution. We advocate for distinguishing between physical and cognitive access as a framework for explaining what the changing communication environment means for our understanding of media effects. Within the PCA framework, we advance a *theory of post-exposure processing* (PEP), which anticipates and explains how and why the affordances and features of communication technologies affect cognitive accessibility with consequences for attention, recall, learning, and persuasion. Our theory offers an important revision to the OMA framework (Prior 2007; Tichenor et al. 1970), a vitally important contribution to the media effects literature as one of the few models that explicitly deals with both pre- and post-exposure factors. Under the logic of OMA, processing and effects from exposure are contingent on ability, conceived as a fixed, individual-level trait. Our framework and theory call attention to the fact that the ability to attend and process information is also conditioned by technological features and affordances of devices and platforms, as well as situational and contextual factors.

According to PEP, digital affordances, platforms, devices, and their features exert their influence on cognitive access through the effects they have on the delivery, presentation, and structure of information—all of which influence individuals' ability to attend and process information. Decades of media effects research have only intermittently taken the effects of information structure seriously, but the work that does makes it very clear that differences in information structure can alter the costs of processing information (Lang 2000; Grabe et al. 2000a; Kim and Sundar 2016). This notion that the "ease" or "costliness" of processing matters is informed by a long-tradition of work in social sciences that finds that costs affect the willingness of individuals to engage in pro-civic behaviors such as information seeking (Downs 1957; Riker and Ordeshook 1968; Lupia and McCubbins 1998; Lau and Redlawsk 2001). Moreover, our theory is consistent with earlier work on the effects of major shifts in communication technology, such as the arrival and expansion of television. The proliferation of television reduced the cost of political information seeking first by expanding physical access to citizens via broadcast signals, and second by limiting programming to news for several hours of every morning and evening. It reduced the cost of political information processing—by increasing cognitive access to news (Grabe et al. 2000b)—because it presented news in a more entertaining and easily understood format, relative to newspapers (Prior 2007). Thus, to the extent that our theory can be applied to other communication technologies, we can use it to better situate new expectations and explanations in the context of what decades of research have told us about media effects.

APPLICATION TO SOCIAL MEDIA AND BEYOND

Our theory is applicable to other advancements in information communication technology. Just as our framework and theory provided the necessary theoretical context with which to understand the effects of expanding access to and use of mobile communication technologies, it can be employed to understand the effects of other devices, platforms, and features in the digital media environment.

For example, we speculate that while social media also vastly expands physical access (and even exposure) to political information (and importantly, non-credible information), the ways in which it structures information are liable to change cognitive access with consequences for attention, learning, and impression formation (Settle 2018; Bode 2016; Thorson and Wells 2016; Thorson et al. 2019; Vraga et al. 2016). Existing work provides some suggestive evidence with respect to these outcomes. Also using eye tracking, Vraga et al. (2014, 2016) find the type of post and topic on Facebook garners different patterns of attention for news posts. This is further evidenced by the quick identification of, and minimal engagement with political Facebook posts the authors document using eye tracking. In a more recent study (2019), they use measures of *selective attention* (as opposed to exposure), to demonstrate the ways Facebook's platform structures visual attention so as to engage otherwise uninterested users. The authors find little evidence of selective exposure based on interest, theorizing that features of the platform and the low cognitive effort required to engage with the content change the relationship between interest and exposure. Both the PCA framework and PEP model are consistent with this logic. Despite higher rates of incidental exposure to political information on social media, we do not observe the similar learning effects from inadvertent exposure to news on television (Bode 2016). Indeed, while Facebook can increase incidental exposure to political information, resulting in agenda-setting effects, these effects do not extend to learning (Feezell and Ortiz 2019).

And just as surely as scholarly optimism gives way to pessimism, a new platform comes along. Take TikTok, another mobile-dominant platform that publishes user-generated short-form videos: physical access to these videos via a mobile device constrains delivery of content in ways that affects post-exposure processing. Additionally, platform affordances, such as algorithmic filtering, make it likely that users only encounter content of interest. Given general disinterest in political posts on other social media platforms (Vraga et al. 2016), it seems unlikely that TikTok is generating large numbers of ideal citizens. On the other hand, the audio-visual nature of this content makes it likely that users are transported (feelings of being there), possibly increasing opportunities for learning.

In the gaming world, our theory is also consistent with findings showing that VR technology transports audiences, resulting in more susceptibility to persuasion (Burrows and Blanton 2016); these effects are likely the result of high cognitive access (Kim and Sundar 2016). And where Burrows and Blanton focus on persuasion, PEP suggests VR can facilitate political learning under the right conditions. Regardless of the device, platform, and outcomes of interest, we hope that the PCA framework and PEP model set forth in this book offers researchers one approach to studying the effects of these emerging platforms.

Are We Entering a New Era of Minimal Effects?

The insights we provide also speak to the debate regarding the new era of minimal effects (Bennett and Iyengar 2008). Our position is that any declarations about a new era of minimal effects are premature. *In fact, we largely attribute anticipation of a new era of minimal effects to media effects researchers' relative neglect of post-exposure processing.* Decades ago, effects researchers' fixation on what communication technologies meant for media effects on political attitude change prolonged the era of minimal effects (Iyengar 2017). Today the key outcomes of interest are partisan affect or polarization, and still the literature depicts these outcomes in the context of political attitude change. Researchers are just as preoccupied with persuasion as they were decades ago, and a possible consequence is premature declarations for a new era of minimal effects.

Given our findings, this argument might seem counterintuitive. After all, we find that in the mobile case, post-exposure processing effects include attenuated attention and decreased learning. If we extend the logic to attitude change, we would expect media messages delivered via mobile to be less likely to persuade due to reduced rates of attention. This extension suggests more support for minimal effects, but that depends on how we define media effects. Our argument is two-fold. First, the "effects" within the study of media effects should encompass more than persuasion. This is largely already the case—there are scores of well-known studies on learning, political knowledge, and participation and on indirect effects, such as agenda-setting, priming, and framing—all of which are widely considered studies of media effects. But when Bennet and Iyengar (2008) posed the question over a decade ago, they did so in the context of media effects' more traditional focus: persuasion. This focus is one reason why an affirmative answer to the question, "are we in a new era of minimal effects?" was plausible.

If we consider an expansive definition of media effects the answer is far less clear. During the broadcast era, inadvertent exposure to television news had learning effects that served to broaden the news audience. Selective exposure to partisan media has conditional effects on learning, engagement, and participation (Prior 2007). These are both example of effects shaped by changes to information communication technology. It would substantially enhance theory-building in media effects if we include political learning and knowledge as media effects, as well as attention, which is important both as a precursor and outcome.

Second, and importantly, we argue that the "media" in media effects should include more than just the message. This includes the content and structure of the message, platform, and delivery, as well as structural features of the information environment. *Thus, we advocate for integrating both market-structural and message-structural effects into our frameworks, such that technological features are central to understanding media effects.* In other words, media effects research should consider effects from device and platform features that shape messages in ways that change their impact as media effects. From this view, we think that media effects are far more likely to be conditional rather than minimal, but this conclusion depends on a more inclusive definition of media effects.

If we take a step back from persuasion, and take attention and learning into consideration we can see that, at least in the mobile case, new communication technologies can shape media messages in ways consequential for media effects because they operate in tandem with situational context to affect attention. We know from the limited amount of work that has considered social media platforms' impact on information structure (Settle 2018) that impression formation is also influenced by the manner in which social media displays and delivers social and political information. Still other work reveals that despite higher rates of incidental exposure on social media, we do not observe the same learning effects from increased incidental exposure to news on television (Vraga et al. 2019). Why? Our theory would suggest its due to the way social media presents and structures political information on news feeds (in snippets and streams co-mingled with social information) in ways that affect post-exposure information processing. Not to mention that so much social media feed scrolling actually occurs on mobile devices, likely compounding the processing challenges of both platform and device. If we consider attention part of the media effects equation, and we should (McGuire 1968; Zaller 1992), then these platforms condition effects. *We argue that by focusing on the effects of the expanding media choice environment and neglecting the importance of post-exposure information processing, we risk once again perpetuating a myth of minimal effects.*

Whither Technological Determinism?

The theoretical arguments, findings, and interpretation of the results presented in this book should not be interpreted as technological determinism. Indeed, our theory is consistent with work on communication technology affordances, which demonstrates that technology facilitates certain behaviors but is not determinative of those behaviors (e.g., Gibson and Carmichael 1966; Evans et al. 2017; Trilling, Tolochko, and Burscher 2017; Matthes et al. 2020). Indeed, the effects of platform and device affordances on post-exposure processing will be contingent on individual characteristics, informational attributes, context, and mode of access. For example, individuals keenly interested in seeking news are unlikely to be undeterred by the information processing costs associated with mobile devices or platforms, and as outlined by the OMA framework, individual-level traits like ability matter, too.

And there are reasons for optimism. First, the news industry has treated this disruption to the communication environment as a means to innovate, taking the unique informational challenges posed by mobile as an opportunity to change presentational styles with regard to information content and structure, which is no small feat for an industry known to be dilatory. While scholars and practitioners may often speak past each other in efforts to better understand news behaviors, the evidence we present here demonstrates a greater need for collaboration: scholars should work to facilitate an understanding of attention commensurate with metrics used in the news industry, and practitioners should consider bringing social science into their user experience designs. Hopefully, over time, research will be able to provide recommendations for the news industry about how to adapt mobile news content in ways that capture and retain the attention of their audience in a complicated information landscape.

Second, the continuing evolution of hardware and infrastructures for communication technology also offers promise. As technological improvements increase wireless speeds, screen sizes, and resolutions, the immersive capabilities of mobile devices will continue to improve and can potentially offset some of the current costs exerted on news consumers. In addition, as platforms proliferate and evolve, at least some software developers will undoubtedly figure out new ways that the display, delivery, and structure of information can sustain attention—even for news. But for now, in a context where news organizations are in a scramble to craft their news content in ways compatible with constraints of the mobile environment, mobile news consumers face a paradox—they have more access to more outlets than ever before—but they may learn less.

Normative Implications

DIGITAL INEQUALITIES

The advent of cable and internet moved the pendulum toward information abundance, making a wide array of sources for news and political information available around-the-clock. The portability of mobile devices and advances in wireless technology extended twenty-four-hour, high-choice access to the individual. Through their portability and affordability, mobile devices expanded physical access to information. However, what is distinct about mobile devices is that the very features enabling expansion of *physical* access to information can also operate to constrain *cognitive* access. Mobile devices make information available to more people at more times throughout the day, but there are functional limitations for news consumption on mobile devices that dissuade attention to news.

Mobile access to the internet provides a lot of opportunity, and it is certainly better than no access. But the shift to mobile also brings more economic disruptions for news outlets and limits the packaging of stories to bits and bytes while imposing serious information-seeking challenges for citizens. Which citizens are most affected will vary over time as connections and data capabilities on mobile devices continue to improve and as news organizations adapt their content to the mobile setting. Yet, the results presented herein paint the possibility of significant societal change: increasing reliance on mobile internet access constrains attention to news in ways that are likely to sharpen information inequities along the lines of political interest, class, race, and ethnicity, further reducing the proportion of the public that can be credibly described as democratically informed and engaged.

Perhaps more insidiously, many individuals who rely on their phones or their tablets to consume information likely do not even realize they spend less time attending to news content. Instead, most users likely believe their mobile devices make accessing news and political information easier. However, *access and exposure are distinct from attention.* The differences between the actual effects of mobile access and the perceptions thereof are why it is so important that we begin to unpack the complicated relationship between user characteristics, device characteristics, and information.

Those in the news industry tasked with creating a decidedly modern product delivered via mobile devices may be concerned that, as currently structured, readers on mobile devices may spend less time on their sites and be less focused on their content. Our results also point to the need for news media to go beyond user experience testing to consider the broader economic *and* normative ramifications of changes to information delivery and presentation. Simply, *in making content more appealing to digital audiences, media may inadvertently be decreasing the long-term value of news.* Given immense concerns about the economic health of news media, these effects, even if small, may be of great consequence. Beyond the immediate consequences mobile has for news consumption, for those interested in information and communication broadly—whether as practitioners or scholars—these results suggest we need to pay more attention to attention (see also Myllylahti 2019).

Our findings qualify the notion that having mobile access to the internet is better than not having access at all. While true, we must recognize the important differences in the affordances of high-speed internet on a traditional computer and access on a mobile device (Mossberger et al. 2013; Napoli and Obar 2014). Of course, the kinds of audiences left without optimal access for digital citizenship will vary over time as connections and data capabilities on mobile devices continue to improve. And yet, in the Unites States case, the policy debate over tiers of access and speed persists, as does the question of affordability. The Federal Communications Commission (FCC) released a study in 2017 which suggested mobile access is a suitable replacement for high-speed internet access (Brodkin 2017). Access to broadband services is variable and cost sensitive, and our work suggests that attention to news will also be a casualty of mobile reliance. Even as laptops shrink and smartphone screens grow, mobility will always necessitate smaller screens and—without a change in FCC tune—connectivity speed differences may also continue. Our results speak broadly to the civic consequences of such shifts.

Academics, journalists, the punditry, and ordinary citizens have sharply focused on the relationship between partisan cleavages and fragmenting media, but we should also be concerned about information cleavages that break across lines of political interest, race, ethnicity, income, occupation, and modes of access to the internet. The public's increasing reliance on mobile internet suggests that the mobile era is here. The negative effects of disproportionate reliance on mobile internet access are evidenced in the difficulties reported by those without high-speed internet access. Younger people, Latinos, African Americans, and individuals with fewer resources more frequently cite the high cost of high-speed broadband as prohibitive and also more frequently report this to be a major impediment in several key areas pertinent to quality of life (Horrigan and Duggan 2015).

Our framework, theoretical arguments, and evidence also clearly support arguments for thinking about digital divides as quality of access rather than a binary (DiMaggio and Hargittai 2001; Lelkes 2020). The level of physical access to information people have structures their cognitive access—the ease with which they seek, serendipitously encounter, and process news. The quality of physical access will have implications for cognitive access, and as we have shown, binary notions of access might be indicative of the opportunity for exposure, but nothing more. That someone has the opportunity for exposure to information does not tell us much about post-exposure information processing.

As made clear by mobile data trends, there is little doubt that mobile connectivity increases physical access to news and political information. Mobile internet access brings the wide world of media choice to our fingertips, at once expanding the availability and array of media choice. Whether access is translating into exposure, attention, and cognitive engagement is another matter entirely.

Is There Any Good News in What We Learn from Mobile News?

While the story is complicated and the normative implications fraught, it is not all bad news. With respect to the application of the framework and theory to the mobile case, we see this work as bracketing the conditions under which mobile internet access is optimal. Better understanding these conditions gives us the opportunity to deploy mobile communication technology and ultimately, we may be able to better leverage mobile affordances for democratically desirable goals. We certainly would not advocate for the end of mobile devices, nor would it be fruitful to do so (what would we do in faculty meetings?). We are careful not to throw out the proverbial baby with the bathwater: we emphasize throughout this book the delimiting factors that shape mobile use, and the circumstances under which mobile devices are best (and least) suited.

There are other potentially overlooked normatively desirable implications from our results, and from the application of our framework and model to the broader category of digital media in particular. First among them are the implications for social media, persuasion, and misinformation. Much scholarly consternation focuses on misinformation (e.g., Lazer et al. 2018). In fact, alarm over misinformation exposure outpaces evidence of its effects (Lewendowsky et al. 2017; Dunaway 2021). There are numerous sound reasons for such concern, but it is important to qualify rates of exposure with the knowledge that that the majority of social media activity takes place on a mobile device (Droesch 2019). Our work suggests that cognitive access to such information, among mobile users on Facebook for example, is likely to be poor, resulting in less attention and ultimately, less recall. Although rates of exposure to misinformation on social media are alarmingly high, the decades of research discussed in Chapters 1 and 2 demonstrate clearly that persuasion requires attention and processing. Thus far, research cannot conclusively determine the extent to which the affordances and features of social media platforms or those of mobile devices encourage or discourage attention and processing. It might be that one reason alarm about misinformation is so high is due to overly narrow focus on exposure and a relative failure to consider their effects on post-exposure processing. Simply put, the PCA framework and PEP model suggest it is quite possible that the persuasive effects of exposure to misinformation among mobile Facebook users will be minimal, just as we might expect their depressive effects on attention, learning and recall to be substantial. Similarly, recent angst over the effects of online political ads and even targeted forms of misinformation (Kim et al. 2018)—also primarily delivered via mobile-first platforms—may be mitigated given the subpar post-exposure processes our model predicts would result on mobile.

However, our relatively optimistic take on mobile receipt and processing of misinformation is tempered by the possibility that the same argument can also be applied to *corrections* to misinformation. In fact, attention to corrections might present more challenges relative to the misinformation itself. Conspiracy theories and "fakes news" are often shared from peers which may increase one's attention to it (e.g., Messing and Westwood 2014) and rumors and misinformation often involves highly emotional or dramatic content that may arouse attention (e.g. Arceneaux et al. 2021) whereas corrections might be "boring" with little attention paid to them especially on mobile devices.

Another thing to consider from a normative perspective is whether we are applying the right standard with regard to the importance of citizen knowledge. Research on information processing adds nuance to our understanding of how citizens engage in a democracy, underscoring that not every citizen needs to (or can) meet the ideals of a well-informed citizenry as described in democratic theory. Although there is a healthy debate on the point, substantial evidence shows that less-informed citizens can use heuristics and other means to arrive at sound decisions (Lupia and McCubbins 1998). Such work would suggest that frequent—even if fleeting—visits to sources for online news on mobile devices might be sufficient for obtaining heuristic information. While we believe this to be true, an important caveat is needed: research shows that less-informed citizens are less likely to use cues in the way that their better-informed peers do (Lau and Redlawsk 2001). Given the digital disparities we outline in Chapter 3, it is possible that those with lower socioeconomic status are the same citizens more likely to depend heavily on their smartphones for internet access, and more likely to report having a hard time keeping up with the news. As long as those patterns persist, it might be those who are least equipped to use heuristics who are also reliant on smartphones as key points of access to public affairs information. More research is needed in order to answer these questions conclusively.

Along similar lines, research on "fire alarms vs. monitorial citizens" (Zaller 2003) suggests that even though many citizens may not regularly monitor the information environment because politics is not important to their daily life, they will do so when important events (a pandemic, a war, an economic crisis, an election) occur. Applying this logic to our findings about mobile news use, it may be that once something important happens, people will pay attention and, moreover, will do so via modes of access more amenable to processing complex information and performing difficult tasks, such as computers or even print media.

In other words, that smartphone use is supplemented, or even replaced, when the situation calls for different informational needs is likely. Still, we believe that, while this may be the case, the possibility of people supplementing traditional media use with smartphone news access does not repudiate the need for more scholarly attention to post-exposure processing broadly, and mobile technology specifically. As we state in Chapter 3, research is not yet clear on the degree to which smartphones and tablets serve as supplemental means by which to seek information or a replacement and for whom. Real-world data speaks to this possibility as well, but provides only mixed evidence. According to OFCOM data on media consumption patterns in the UK, there does not appear to have been much of a shift in consumption during the pandemic. If anything, the growth of new mobile-dominated platforms such as TikTok point in the other direction. The most popular online platform in the UK right now is WhatsApp, which is mobile-centric and used by seventy-two percent of the adult public (up from forty-five percent in 2018). According to Pew data from August and September of 2020, more than eight-in-ten Americans get news from digital devices, and sixty percent say that they do so often.[2] That so many people were getting their news on smartphones and tablets in the midst of a global pandemic and a contentious presidential election might be indicative, but the Pew data do not rule out supplemental use—reliance on smartphones in addition to computers, television, or other platforms.

Another issue is that in many homes and educational settings, smartphones and tablets are replacing traditional computers. Many homes that would have had computers five years ago do not have them at all today, preventing their emergent use. In both the United States and in the United Kingdom, there are major concerns about the lack of computer access playing a role in education inequalities during the pandemic. Nevertheless, for those citizens who are not dependent on mobile devices for access to the internet, it is possible that they might reserve their more intense bouts of information seeking on important topics for times and locations in which they need not rely on their cellphones. More work is needed to be able to understand when, how, and why people access information via different modes, and the consequences thereof.

Conclusion

In this book we sought to add to the current body of knowledge about what recent and evolving communication technologies mean for media effects. Contingents of politicians, pundits, journalists, citizens, and researchers are often wary of what drastic changes to the information environment could mean—whether it be for political persuasion, the economics of the news business, or everyday citizens' ability to stay informed. This is still true, and media effects research has a decades-long history to show for it. As we tried to illustrate here, there is still much we can learn from past research on media effects, despite the rather dramatic changes that characterized the media environment over the last few decades.

Substantively, we hope that this book demonstrates that the means by which communication technologies exert influence remain largely the same, even as the affordances and features of the devices and platforms continue to change. Communication technologies have an impact on media effects because they shape both physical and cognitive access to information. When viewed through this framework, it becomes clear how focusing primarily on those changes that structure the opportunity to consume various kinds of political news and information (i.e., on pre-exposure processes) tells only part of the story. While exposure is necessary for both persuasion and learning, it is not sufficient without attention. And a large part of how technology exerts its impact is in how it invites or curbs attention once exposure occurs. Thus, we hope that the PEP theory and its application to the mobile case motivates more scholars to take-up the challenge of understanding how communication technologies structure attention in an increasingly digital, social, and mobile media world.

Given our contention that much post-broadcast effects research on post-exposure processes is limited due to methodological challenges, we also hope that our use of psychophysiological methods and measures in the lab, coupled with real-world web-traffic data outside the lab, will further advance research. This is important because much more work needs to be done. Although we apply them usefully here in the effort to shed light on post-exposure processing, future research that can better integrate both pre- and post-exposure processes into research designs will go much further to help us understand how technology shapes both physical and cognitive access to information. Future work should also try to more fully understand the many possible contextual effects on attention and processing. In part because it is difficult to study, the field knows very little about how people weave information seeking and consumption on mobile devices into their daily lives and what effects the different contexts in which they consume information will have on patterns of attention to information and processing. Furthermore, we desperately need to learn more about the extent to which mobile devices replace former modes of information seeking or whether their use is supplemental. Whatever the case may be, we need to know whether those patterns ameliorate or further information inequalities and divides in political participation. It may be the case that there is an important division of labor emerging in which people who are politically interested, knowledgeable, and engaged benefit from fixed modes of access but then use their mobile devices to *extend* that engagement offline via the organizational affordances of mobile access (protest, citizen journalism, neighborhood politics, movement coordination). Such patterns might contribute to the divides we identify in Chapter 3.

The studies we report in this book tell us a great deal about how affordances and features of devices shape attention and learning. Yet our framework and theory offer promise for informing many other studies. In this book we only scratch the surface with regard to the outcomes examined. Future work should investigate effects on persuasion and attitude change as well as behavioral outcomes such as click-through rates, liking, and sharing digital political information. And, as our discussion above suggests, future work should also examine the effects of other devices, platforms, and features, and it should do so across various informational contexts reflective of the real-world settings in which information exposure and consumption takes place.

Post-broadcast media effects research is enormously valuable in telling us how the structure of the information environment allows for an active audience. Active audiences—through the many choices they are afforded—are sometimes thought to be more or less susceptible to media effects depending on whether the nature of their exposure to media is motivated or inadvertent. But what we show here, also implied by our framework and theory, is that the changing information environment exerts influence on the kinds of content to which people are exposed through more ways than just its constraints on physical access to information or media choice. The affordances and features of platforms and devices also exert influence on content, namely by shaping the structure of information. These effects on information structure are those likely to exert their impact on post-exposure processing. And while our research does not rule out the possibility that effects on post-exposure processing can operate in tandem with motivations for news exposure, we demonstrate effects on cognitive access independent of whether exposure is motivated or inadvertent. Much more research is needed before we can fully understand media effects in a digital, social, and mobile era. We hope our framework and theory—which builds on extant research spanning several disciplines and subfields—can help guide some of that future work.

Supplementary Information and Methodological Details

Chapter 3

Table A3.1 **OLS models predicting audience reach (Study 5)**

	Audience Reach (Model 1)	*Audience Reach* (Model 2)
Tablet	−0.05 (0.008)***	−0.03 (0.008)***
Smartphone	0.27 (0.02)***	0.25 (0.02)***
App	—	−0.27 (0.07)***
Constant	0.3 (0.027)***	0.3 (0.03)***
N	915	986
R-Squared	0.06	0.06

Note: Entries are coefficients from OLS regression models with standard errors clustered by news outlet in parentheses. Due to departures from normality reach is logged. The comparison group for device use is computer.

* $p < 0.05$, ** $p < 0.01$, *** $p < 0.001$, two-tailed tests.

Table A3.2 **Log-gamma GLM models predicting audience reach (Study 5)**

	Audience Reach	Audience Reach
	(Model 1)	(Model 2)
Tablet	−0.28 (0.04)***	−0.21 (0.04)***
Smartphone	0.96 (0.04)***	0.90 (0.04)***
App	—	−0.82 (0.04)*
Constant	−0.44 (0.17)**	−0.44 (0.17)**
N	915	986
Wald χ^2	900.74***	815.03***
D/ϕ	2.70	2.85

Note: We also specify an alternative model that models the non-normal data generating process. Above are estimates from a log-gamma GLM with standard errors clustered by news outlet in parentheses. The comparison group for device use is computer. * $p < 0.05$, ** $p < 0.01$, *** $p < 0.001$, two-tailed tests.

Chapter 4

STUDY 1 DETAILS

This study was approved by LSU's Institutional Review Board. Two trained research associates administered the test. Participants over the age of eighteen were invited to participate in studies for extra credit. Recruits choose among

Table A4.1 **Sample details by study**

Study	N	Date, Location	Demographics
Study 1	115	March–April 2015, LSU Media Effects Lab	Age M = 20.2 years; 87 women, 28 men; 88 White, 27 non-Whites; 33 Democrats/leaners, 62 Republicans/leaners, and 20 Independents
Study 2	56	February 2016, LSU Media Effects Lab	Age M = 20.4 years; 50 women, 5 men; 38 White, 18 non-Whites; 17 Democrats/leaners, 23 Republicans/leaners, 15 Independents, 1 non-response
Study 3	892	May 2015, Amazon MTurk	Age M= 34.27 years; 388 women, 465 men; 670 White, 184 non-Whites; 401 Democrats/leaners, 144 Republicans/leaners, and 281 Independents
Study 4	113	August–May 2016, UM & Texas A&M	Age M = 19.6 years; 86 women, 27 men; 51 Southern, 62 Midwestern.
Study 5	3,285	Comscore	—

Table A4.2 **Variables, measurements, and descriptive statistics (Study 1, 2)**

		Study 1, 2 (Eye Tracking Studies)	
Treatments	*Measurement*	*Descriptive Statistics*	
		Study 1	Study 2
Device Use	Device participants used.	0 = Computer (33.0%) 1 = Tablet (31.3%) 2 = Smartphone (35.7%)	0 = Computer (50%) 1 = Tablet (50%)
News Type	Type of news story.	—	0 = Ent (53.6%) 1 = News (46.4%)
Reading Time	Time participants spent fixated on the news story; measured in seconds and captured by eye tracker.	Cronbach's α = 0.89 Range: 0–85.72 M = 28.44 SD = 23.54	Cronbach's α = 0.84 Range: 0.71–136.94 M = 66.34 SD = 33.87
Duration of Link Fixations	The duration of all fixations on link(s); in seconds.	Range: 0–4.65 M = 0.56 SD = 0.83	Range: 0–10.48 M = 1.9 SD = 2.24
Counts of Link Fixations	The number of times the participant fixates on links.	Range: 0–17 M = 2.37 SD = 3.36	Range: 0–27 M = 7.86 SD = 8.05
Noticed Link(s)	Dummy for whether participants fixated on links.	0 = No (38.9%) 1 = Yes (61.1%)	0 = No (25%) 1 = Yes (75%)
Recall	Correct responses to three posttest questions about the news story (Study 1); total number of details recalled (Study 2).	Range: 0–3 M = 2.46 SD = 0.69	Range: 0–9 M = 4.2 SD = 2.19
Recall 24-hours later	Total number of details recalled when asked via Qualtrics open-ended survey question 24-hours after treatment delivery.	—	Range: 0–8 M = 3.47 SD = 1.87
Cognitive Effort	Averaged right and left pupil size during exposure to stimulus.	Range: 0.84–1.63 M = 1.24 SD = 0.14	Range: 0.77–1.63 M = 1.14 SD = 0.17

available survey modes and times in advance of participation. The survey was advertised as a study on news consumption. Students were informed that the study would take about fifteen minutes, during which time they would read a news story and respond to related questions. Upon arrival to the lab, participants first completed a pre-test questionnaire measuring political orientation, habitual media use, and general media trust. As part of the pre-test informed consent was obtained from the participants. They were then asked to read a news story stimulus on their assigned device. Participants were advised to take their time reading; there was no time limit. In the post-test questionnaire, participants were asked open- and close-ended questions about the news story they were assigned to read. We employed haphazard as-if random assignment

Table A4.3 **Randomization check (Study 1)**

	Treatment
Computer	
Age	1.02 (3.03)
Men	−0.11 (0.53)
White	0.29 (0.58)
Democrat	−0.01 (0.75)
Republican	−0.14 (0.78)
Ideology	−0.05 (0.19)
High Political Interest	0.13 (0.50)
Tablet	
Age	2.42 (2.96)
Men	−0.71 (0.59)
White	0.53 (0.64)
Democrat	−1.03 (0.79)
Republican	−0.83 (0.8)
Ideology	0.16 (0.21)
High Political Interest	1.50 (0.52)*
N	115
Wald χ^2	10.06
Prob > χ^2	0.76
Pseudo R^2	0.04

Note: Table features multinomial logit results predicting device treatment; smartphone is reference category. The omitted reference group is "Independent" for party identification. Standard Errors in parentheses. * $p < 0.05$, two-tailed tests.

Table A4.4 **ANOVA models predicting attention to news and links (Study 1)**

Outcome Variables	All Conditions	Tablet vs. Computer	Smartphone vs. Computer	Smartphone vs. Tablet
		Pairwise Comparisons		
Reading Time	$F(2,106) = 69.51***$	diff = −1.55***	diff = −1.14***	diff = 0.40
Counts of Link Fixations	$F(2,106) = 6.03**$	diff = −2.58**	diff = −1.79**	diff = 0.79
Duration of Link Fixations	$F(2,106) = 5.08**$	diff = −0.61**	diff = −0.35	diff = 0.26

Note: *** $p < 0.001$, ** $p < 0.01$.

to sort participants into one of three conditions: computer, tablet, or smartphone condition. Dynamic coding was used to account for scrolling. We use data from all respondents.

STUDY 2 DETAILS

This study was approved by LSU's Institutional Review Board. Two trained research associates administered the test. Recruits chose among available survey modes and times in advance of participation. The survey was advertised as a study

Table A4.5 **Randomization check (Study 2)**

	Treatment
Age (logged)	−10.60 (5.59)
Men	0.02 (1.32)
White	−2.22 (1.00)*
Democrat	−1.47 (1.20)
Republican	−2.68 (1.29)*
Ideology	−0.14 (0.36)
High Political Interest	−1.50 (0.91)
N	49
Wald χ^2	16.57
Prob > χ^2	0.0204
Pseudo R^2	0.2441

Note: Table features binary logit results predicting (a) device treatment (computer = 1, tablet = 0). The omitted reference group is "Independent" for party identification. Standard Errors in parentheses. * $p < 0.05$, two-tailed tests.

on news consumption. Students were informed that the study would take about thirty minutes, during which time they would read a news story and respond to related questions. Upon arrival to the lab, participants first completed a pre-test questionnaire measuring political orientation, habitual media use, and general media trust. As part of the pre-test informed consent was obtained from the participants. They were then asked to read a news story stimulus on their assigned device. Participants were advised to take their time reading; there was no time limit. In the post-test questionnaire, participants were asked open- and close-ended questions about the news story they were assigned to read. We employed random assignment to sort participants into one of two conditions: computer or tablet.

For this study we also manipulated content type into hard news versus entertainment. To ensure comparability, we leveraged a news article about presidential candidate Donald Trump's appearance as host on *Saturday Night Live*, emphasizing political groups' involvement in the hard news condition and removing that emphasis in the entertainment condition. While approaching the stimulus this design required a trade-off between story comparability and a subtle manipulation, given the importance of precise measurement at this point in our testing we opted for the former. Drawing on an actual news article attributed to author Seth Abramovitch, we interchanged the words "heckle" (entertainment condition) and "protest" (news condition) to describe a group's interference as a subtle content type manipulation. Because the manipulation failed, analyses were combined. The stimulus was designed so that no scrolling was required.

STUDY 3 DETAILS

Study 3 received Institutional Review Board approval at Louisiana State University. Study 3 was conducted entirely online using Qualtrics to field the survey and Amazon's MTurk to recruit participants. Workers who were already registered on MTurk could opt to participate in the experiment from a list of Human Intelligence Tasks (HITs). Respondents were instructed to enter their MTurk code at the end of the survey to receive payment. We also placed restrictions on the HIT such that only workers who met the following requirements could see the HIT: eighteen years or older, citizen of the United States, at least a ninety-five percent approval rating, and completion of at least one thousand HITS. We also set restrictions so that no respondent would be able to re-take the survey. We paid all respondents the promised amount. In the online instructions, participants were told that this study was interested in their media consumption and media attitudes and would take about fifteen minutes to complete. They

Table A4.6 **Variables, measurements, and descriptive statistics (Study 3)**

Study 3 (Online Labor Market Study)		
Treatment	*Measurement*	*Descriptive Statistics*
Device Use	Device participants used.	0 = Computer (85.5%) — 1 = Mobile (14.5%)
Recall	Correct responses to three posttest questions about the news story.	Range: 0–3 — M = 2.55 SD = 0.68
Reading Time	Time participants spent on reading the news story; measured in seconds and captured by Qualtrics.	Range: 2.53–17106.63 — M = 97.38 SD = 602.02

were also told that they would be asked to read a news story and answer related questions afterward. We excluded eighty-one cases due to patterned responses, which is a data screening method for identifying careless responders (Meade and Craig 2012). To check for patterned response, we followed Johnson's (2005) LongString index to identify consecutive items (a) with the same response option chosen (e.g., 1,1,1,1 on a Likert scale for four items), as well as (b) with the same difference between two consecutive items (e.g., 1,2,1,2,3,2 on a Likert scale for six items). Eventually, the total number of absolute 0s is computed for each respondent using these two rules. A cutoff value of thirty was chosen based on clear break points in a frequency distribution of raw data.

Participants were given two options: to read a hard news story on politics or to read an entertainment story. Both options were accompanied by pictures of one of the people quoted in the story. Once participants proceeded to the next page, they saw the text of the story they selected along with a headline (see Figure 4.4). The hard news story used in this study was the same news article on gender pay gap used in Study 1, although the recommended links differed. We offered three story topics that appeared to be hyperlinked: economy, sports, and crime. Like the previous study, these hyperlinks were not active. They were mainly used to measure the respondents' second-level choice of news topic. The entertainment story was about the possible revival of a popular 1980s television show and was chosen by using search keywords "Home Improvement show," and "entertainment news." It had the same three-story links as the hard news story. Both stories were similar in length and used very similar pictures—an upper-torso portrait for one person. Like the hard news story, material for the entertainment story was sourced from the web and was crafted to match standard entertainment write-ups by a former news reporter.

STUDY 4 DETAILS

This experiment is modeled on one originally fielded by Soroka and McAdams (2015). In light of recent work illustrating that viewing angle, and not just screen size, affect responses (Bellman et al. 2009; Hou et al. 2012), we note that our laptop manipulation required that participants sit at roughly fixed distances from the screen. Although participants were instructed they could shift in their seats as needed for comfort, they were seated at a desk, on a chair without wheels, with their fingers connected by wires to an encoder that sat on the table in a way that set respondents' bodies about six to eight inches from the edge of the table. (The palm of the respondents' hand was placed just over the edge of the table, in front of the encoder.) Participants were unable to move the laptop or themselves around enough to significantly affect viewing angle. Physiological data were gathered using a ProComp encoder, skin conductance sensor, and blood volume pulse sensor from Thought Technology. The manipulation most critical to this study is the random assignment of participants to either large- or small-screen conditions. Screen size is thus a between-subjects factor, while story tone (negative and positive) is a within-subjects factor. We manipulate screen size while holding all else constant to ensure we accurately estimate the impact of screen size on reactions to news stories. The randomization was implemented by flipping a coin for each participant. Story selection is discussed in more detail in Soroka and McAdams (2015). BBC stories are used exclusively as the original purpose of the experiment on which ours was modeled was to field a broadly cross-national study on news negativity. Story selection was guided by the need to capture a range of stories that would be, in any combination, a reasonable approximation of an evening newscast. There are more international stories than in the typical newscast, but this is because stories were also selected to be relatively timeless so that they could be fielded at any time. We account for the potentially arousing nature of stories by coding them for positive and negative tone, and this sentiment coding is critical to ensuring that the effects we observe in our other chapters are not an artifact of the interesting or uninteresting nature of the news story stimuli, and because previous work shows the important effects news story tone can have on audience cognitive and emotional engagement (Soroka 2014; Soroka and McAdams 2015). Tone is a binary measure based on codes by experts and researchers. Note that the results indicate that expert coders' assessments are in line with those from experimental participants: the final column of Table 4.1 shows the mean score for negativity, on a scale from 1 to 7, based on a post-experiment question asking participants to

Table A4.7 **Variables, measurements, and descriptive statistics (Study 4)**

Study 4 (Skin Conductance and Heart Rate Variability)		
Screen Size (Between-Subjects)	Size of Window Used to Display Video News Story. Small = roughly 4.5 inches, Large = 13 inches.	0 = Large Screen (53) 1 = Small Screen (50)
Story Tone (Within-subject)	A simple binary coding, based on codes by the researchers and expert coders. Mean Neg is story average for Negativity (where −2 is most positive and +2 is most negative), based on second-by-second coding of each video, averaged across three expert coders.	See Table 4.1.
SCL	The mean of "normalized" SCL across all seven stories, where "normalizing" SCL involves measuring all stimulus-period SCL relative to SCL during each prior inter-stimulus interval. Higher normalized SCL is taken to indicate greater levels of arousal.	Range: −1.25–6.101 $M = 0.701$ $SD = 1.344$
HRV (SDNN)	The standard deviation of the NN intervals (SDNN), calculated over each news story.	Range: 41.288–178.062 $M = 108.777$ $SD = 32.170$
HRV (RMSSD)	Root Mean Square of the Successive Differences (RMSSD); that is, the square root of the mean squared differences of successive NN intervals, calculated over each news story.	Range: 35.544–229.344 $M = 128.809$ $SD = 43.577$
Negativity	Captured by estimating a simple time-series model for each participant, where "normalized" SCL for every 1-second interval is regressed on the overall tone of the video, saving the coefficient for Negativity.	Range: −1.830–1.289 $M = −0.004$ $SD = 0.327$

rate each story for negativity. The correlation between the mean second-by-second score from expert coders and the mean story-level score from participants is .95. This gives us a high degree of confidence in the negativity scores assigned to our experimental stimuli.

STUDY 5 DETAILS

Table A4.8 **Variables, measurements, and descriptive statistics (Study 5)**

	Study 5 (Web Traffic Study)		
Treatment	*Measurement*	*Descriptive Statistics*	*Source*
Device Use	The device of access.	0 = Computer (27%) 1 = Tablet (36.5%) 2 = Smartphone (36.5%)	Comscore
News	Whether the website is news or entertainment.	0 = Entertainment (51.5%) 1 = News (48.5%)	Three coders
App	Access via application or browser.	0 = Browser (86.2%) 1 = APP (13.8%)	Comscore
Average Minutes Per Visitor	Avg. minutes spent on the website, per visitor.	Range: 0–3842.97 $M = 28.98$ $SD = 153.32$	Comscore
Average Minutes Per Visit	The average minutes on the website, per visit.	Range: 0.03–82.00 $M = 2.27$ $SD = 2.26$	Comscore
Reach	Percentage of the audience reached by mode of access.	Range: 0.006–59.5 $M = 0.91$ $SD = 3.41$	Comscore

Chapter 5

Table A5.1 **Models predicting attention to news and links (Study 1)**

	Reading Time (Model 1)	Duration of Link Fixations (Model 2)	Counts of Link Fixations (Model 3)	Noticed Link (Model 4)
Tablet	−40.11 (3.70)***	−.61 (0.19)**	−1.15 (0.35)**	−1.89 (0.57)**
Smartphone	−33.83 (4.10)***	−.35 (0.18) +	−0.65 (0.33) +	−1.49 (0.55)**
Constant	52.31 (3.43)***	0.86 (0.13)***	1.33 (0.24)***	1.64 (0.45)***
N	109	109	109	108
F	58.75	5.08	—	—
R²	0.57	0.09	—	—
Wald χ^2	—	—	10.98**	13.85**
D/ϕ	—	—	0.63	—
Pseudo R²	—	—	—	0.10

Note: Models 1 and 2 are OLS, Model 3 is a log-gamma GLM, and Model 4 is a Logit. For each model standard errors are in parentheses; Model 1 standard errors are robust. The comparison group for device use is computer.

+ $p<.1$, * $p < 0.05$, ** $p < 0.01$, *** $p < 0.001$, two-tailed tests.

Table A5.2 **Models predicting attention to news and links (Study 2)**

	Reading Time (Model 1)	Duration of Link Fixations (Model 2)	Counts of Link Fixations (Model 3)	Noticed Link (Model 4)
Tablet	−0.49 (9.14)	−1.72 (0.56)**	−0.80 (0.10)***	−3.15 (1.09)**
Constant	66.59 (6.46) ***	2.77 (0.39)***	2.38 (0.06)***	3.30 (1.02)**
N	56	56	56	56
F	0.00	9.59	—	—
R²	0.0001	0.15	—	—
Wald χ^2	—	—	60.80***	15.68***
D/ϕ	—	—	0.64	—
Pseudo R²	—	—	—	0.25

Note: Models 1 and 2 are OLS, Model 3 is a log-gamma GLM, and Model 4 is a Logit. For each model standard errors are in parentheses. The comparison group for device use is computer.
* $p < 0.05$, ** $p < 0.01$, *** $p < 0.001$, two-tailed tests.

Chapter 6

Table A6.1 **Models predicting HRV and SCL (Study 4)**

	HRV		SCL	
	SDNN	*RMSSD*	*Overall Levels*	*Negativity*
Small Videos	−12.023[+] (6.260)	−20.396* (8.392)	−0.063 (0.269)	−0.116[+] (0.064)
Constant	114.613** (4.362)	138.710** (5.847)	0.739*** (0.186)	0.051 (0.045)
N	103	103	102	102
Rsq	.035	.055	.001	.031

Note: Models are OLS regression. For each model standard errors are in parentheses. [+] $p < 0.1$; *$p < 0.05$; **$p < 0.01$; ***$p < 0.001$, two-tailed tests.

Chapter 7

STUDY 1 DETAILS

Recall in this study indicates the total number of correct answers participants give to the following three questions: "In terms of the news article you've just read ... What was the main issue it talked about?" "What is Marco Rubio's main opinion on that issue?" and "What were the reasons for Marco Rubio mentioned for his position on that issue?" More details on measures and sample details can be found in Table A4.1 and A4.2.

Table A7.1 **OLS Regression model predicting cognitive effort (Study 1)**

	Cognitive Effort
Tablet	0.10 (0.0006)***
Smartphone	0.16 (0.0006)***
Constant	1.16 (0.0004)***
N	362,609
F	36612.32***
R^2	0.17

Note: Outcome variable is the logged averaged pupil size of two eyes. Entries are coefficients with standard errors in parentheses. The comparison group for tablet user and smartphone user is computer user. *$p < 0.05$, **$p < 0.01$, ***$p < 0.001$, two-tailed tests.

Table A7.2 **Poisson regression model predicting recall (Study 1)**

	Recall
Tablet	1.38 (0.16)***
Smartphone	0.99 (0.16)***
Constant	−3.08 (0.11)***
Offset	1
N	92
Wald χ^2	79.03***
Pseudo R^2	0.17

Note: The offset variable is ln(*Reading Time*), with its coefficient set to 1. Entries are coefficients with standard errors in parentheses. The comparison group for tablet user and smartphone user is computer user. *$p < 0.05$, ** $p < 0.01$, *** $p < 0.00$, two-tailed tests.

STUDY 2 DETAILS

In Study 2, *Recall* is conceptualized as how many details a participant recalls immediately after exposure to the story. Participants were instructed: "Please list all the details—minor or major—that you recall from the article in the text box below. Do not worry too much about grammar, spelling, or structure—just list everything that you remember. Take your time! And write as much as you want." Second, we create a variable *Recall 24-hours Later*, which captures how many details a participant recalls twenty-four hours after exposure to the story. In an email, participants were informed that they were being contacted as part of a follow-up to the study and offered additional extra credit for answering additional questions via a Qualtrics online survey. Upon clicking the link, participants were directed: "You may recall reading an article on Trump's appearance on SNL—we are interested in what you recall from that article. If you don't recall very much that is ok, we just want to know anything you may remember. Again, we are just interested in what you remember—so it is very important you don't search for information outside of this page or you may jeopardize our data." Participants ($N = 30$) were then again instructed to list as many things as they could remember from the article. For both *Recall* and *Recall 24-hours Later*, a trained coder counted the number of details provided by each participant. A second trained coder analyzed a ten percent draw of these responses, yielding an acceptable level of inter-coder reliability. According to best practices, we set forth a minimum acceptable level of reliability at .8 for Krippendorf's Alpha, a conservative index. We achieve this standard for both measures. More measure and sample details can be found in Table A4.1 and Table A4.2.

Table A7.3 **OLS regression model predicting cognitive effort (Study 2)**

	Cognitive Effort
Tablet	0.10 (0.04)*
Constant	1.09 (0.03)***
N	56
F	5.52*
R^2	0.09

Note: Outcome variable is the logged averaged pupil size of two eyes. Entries are coefficients with standard errors in parentheses. The comparison group is computer user. *$p < 0.05$, ** $p < 0.01$, *** $p < 0.001$, two-tailed tests.

Table A7.4 **Poisson regression model predicting recall (Study 2)**

	Recall
Tablet	−0.05 (0.13)
Constant	−2.73 (0.09)***
Offset	1
N	56
Wald χ^2	0.16
Pseudo R^2	0.0005

Note: The offset variable is ln(*Reading Time*), with its coefficient set to 1. Entries are coefficients with standard errors in parentheses. The comparison group is computer user. *$p < 0.05$, ** $p < 0.01$, *** $p < 0.001$, two-tailed tests.

Table A7.5 **Poisson regression model predicting recall 24 hours later (Study 2)**

	Recall 24-hours Later
Tablet	−.45 (0.21)*
Constant	−2.83 (0.12)***
Offset	1
N	30
Wald χ^2	4.79*
Pseudo R^2	0.03

Note: The offset variable is ln(*Reading Time*), with its coefficient set to 1. Entries are coefficients with standard errors in parentheses. The comparison group is computer user. *$p < 0.05$, ** $p < 0.01$, *** $p < 0.001$, two-tailed tests.

STUDY 3 DETAILS

Similar to Study 1, *Recall* captures the number of correct recalls participants give to three post-test questions (see Table A4.6 for measure details). As Study 3 employs two stimuli, an entertainment and news story, respondents who choose to read the political news story were asked: "In terms of the news article you've just read . . . What was the primary subject of the policy debate in the article?" "Was Marco Rubio for or against the proposed policy?" and "What was the reason Marco Rubio mentioned for his position on that issue?" On the other hand, for those who self-selected the entertainment story, they were asked: "In terms of the news article you've just read . . . What was the primary subject of the news article?" "Who came up with the idea mentioned in the story?" and "Did the character Al (played by Richard Karn) agree with the others on the issue mentioned in the story?"

Table A7.6 **Poisson regression model**
predicting recall (Study 3)

	Recall
Mobile	0.18 (0.06)**
Constant	−3.70 (0.02)***
Offset	1
N	790
Wald χ^2	7.15**
Pseudo R^2	0.002

Note: The offset variable is ln(*Reading Time*), with its coefficient set to 1. Entries are coefficients with standard errors in parentheses. The comparison group for *Mobile* (including tablet and smartphone) is computer. *$p < 0.05$, ** $p < 0.01$, *** $p < 0.001$, two-tailed tests.

Chapter 8

Table A8.1 **Average minutes per visitor and visit spent on news sites/apps (Study 5)**

	Minutes Per Visitor Browser and App Users (Model 1)	*Minutes Per Visitor Browser Users Only (Model 2)*	*Minutes Per Visit Browser Users Only (Model 3)*
Tablet	−2.84 (0.62)***	−2.84 (0.62)***	−0.11 (0.09)
Smartphone	−6.45 (0.68)***	−6.44 (0.68)***	−0.71 (0.09) ***
App	83.33 (14.32)***	—	—
Constant	10.65 (0.83)***	10.65 (0.83)***	2.42 (0.1)***
N	986	915	915
F	—	52.23***	108.17***
R^2	—	0.06	0.07
Wald χ^2	104.90***		
D/ϕ	0.67		

Note: Model 1 is an identity-gamma GLM; Model 2 and 3 are OLS. Standard errors (clustered on news outlets) are in parentheses. The comparison group for tablets and smartphones is computers. Missing values reflect points of access that did not meet Comscore minimum reporting standards for March 2016. * $p < 0.05$, ** $p < 0.01$, *** $p < 0.001$, two-tailed tests.

Notes

Chapter 1

1. We are grateful to an anonymous reviewer for helping us clarify this important point.
2. Political communication scholars have been guilty of some neglect when it comes to studying post exposure processing; although, there are exceptions, notably: Grabe and Kamwahi (2006); Soroka (2014); Wang et al. (2014); Soroka and McAdams (2015); Trussler and Soroka (2014); Soroka et al. (2016); and Vraga et al. (2016). However, the broader class of media effects researchers have incorporated post-exposure processes into their work, especially when pertinent to the effects of various affordances and features of communication technology. For a helpful discussion see Potter and Bolls (2011); Lang et al. (1995); Lang et al. (1999); Grabe et al. (2000a); Kim and Sundar (2016); Alhabash et al. (2018).
3. In fact, if we limit the political implications of mobile internet access to its effects on physical access to information—the media environment—we can say the same thing. The shift to mobile, if it truly expands the sphere of physical access to information by opening an additional path of access, could be assumed to simply compound the effects of a high media choice environment.
4. Mass communication researchers' interest in the structural features of television news extended to the mid-2000s, and interest in the effects of information structure on both learning and persuasion is clear in emerging lines of research on gaming (Hou et al. 2012) and virtual reality (Burrows and Blanton 2016).
5. This conceptualization of attention motivates our theory which is why our model name—post-exposure processing—is a nod to this work.
6. Recent evidence from the 2016 CCES survey indicates steep increases in the number of survey respondents opting to answer questions on smartphones (Ansolabehere and Schaffner 2017). We think it's fair to extend these trends to labor markets like Mechanical Turk users as well.

Chapter 2

1. We also note that the fragmented state of the literature on the effects of mobile, and communication technology more generally, is also undoubtedly due to the numerous and diverse disciplinary perspectives from which researchers are approaching these questions.
2. In fact, viewed solely through the lens of physical access, we largely agree that nothing about the shift to mobile should make us deviate from the expectation of a new era of minimal effects (Bennett and Iyengar 2008).
3. Each of these metrics are precursors to the likelihood of clicking a link and are proxies for click-through rates.

Chapter 3

1. Countries in Pew's Global Attitudes Survey sample include the United States, Canada, France, Germany, Greece, Hungary, Italy, the Netherlands, Poland, Spain, Sweden, the United Kingdom, Russia, Australia, China, India, Indonesia, Japan, the Philippines, South Korea, Vietnam, Israel, Jordan, Lebanon, Tunisia, Turkey, Ghana, Kenya, Nigeria, Senegal, South Africa, Tanzania, Argentina, Brazil, Chile, Colombia, Mexico, Peru, and Venezuela.
2. Predicted values are based on ordinary least squares (OLS) regression models. Due to the structure of Comscore data, the unit of analysis is the media outlet. The units of observation are the points of access to the outlets' web content, which are based on website visit data from computers, tablets, and smartphones. For example, there are five observations for cnn.com: cnn.com-computer-browser, cnn.com-tablet-browser, cnn.com-tablet-app, cnn.com-smartphone-browser, and cnn.com smartphone-app. These observations are nested within digital outlet. We cluster our standard errors by news outlet.
3. We model these outcomes as a function of three predictors. The first *Tablet* and the second *Smartphone* are dummy variables recoded from a three-category indicator of audience mode of access to the site where 1 = computer, 2 = tablet, and 3 = smartphone, recorded by Comscore. We also include an additional variable *App*, which captures whether individuals access news/entertainment outlet sites via application (coded as 1) or via a web browser (coded as 0). Presently our analyses do not differentiate between operating systems or device brand (i.e., iPhone, Android), nor do we partition audiences according to any demographic categories. The dependent variables are logged.
4. See Chapter 8 for more analyses using the Comscore data.

Chapter 4

1. One recent exception is work by Vraga and colleagues (2019) which uses eye tracking to find that close-ended self-report recall measures are not associated with visual attention to news posts, but they are associated with social and political posts (Vraga et al. 2019), underscoring the need for further study.
2. ICR statistics reported in Chapter 8.

Chapter 6

1. The study presented in this chapter also appears in Dunaway and Soroka (2021).
2. This view of engagement has much in common with "attention" with regard to being about more than simple exposure (see, e.g., Chaffee and Schlueder 1986; Thorson et al. 1985).
3. Testing these explanations applies insights from the literature on screens size (e.g., Lombard et al. 1997) to engage with research on mobile effects on digital citizenship (Napoli and Obar 2014) and recent work on news negativity (e.g., Soroka and McAdams 2015).
4. Note that this randomization means that respondents see varying numbers of positive and negative stories—from two negative and five positive to the opposite, five negative and two positive.
5. Recent work raises questions about the effectiveness and importance of balance testing (Mutz et al. 2019). Even so, randomization checks do not suggest any significant issues where balance is concerned. For instance: small-screen respondents were seventy-seven percent female, while large-screen respondents were seventy-eight percent female; the average age of small-screen respondents was 19.3, while it was 19.8 for large-screen respondents.
6. For the same reason, we are not troubled by the relatively low R-square values in the models shown in Table A6.1. Psychophysiological measures are relatively noisy, we do not expect to account for a good deal of the variance.

Chapter 7

1. Because we allow participants to select the device on which to take the study, they self-assign to treatment (as opposed to being randomized assigned to a treatment), making this a non-equivalent groups quasi-experimental design. One way to deal with possible non-equivalence between groups in these designs is to try to choose treatment and control groups that are as similar to each other as possible (Trochim, Donnelly, and Arora 2016). Lacking the ability to do that here, we conducted a supplementary analysis in which we limited the analysis to matched treatment and control groups. The results presented here are robust to that specification.

Chapter 8

1. Comscore collects web traffic data used in numerous studies (Nelson and Lei 2018). We use two panels: (1) Media Metrix, which tracks desktop traffic; and (2) Mobile Metrix, which tracks traffic from tablets and smartphone via browsers and apps. Desktop tracking occurs through background software for the same users over-time, about one million participants, recording visits to URLs. The mobile panel is approximately twenty thousand adults.

2. Analyses include news sites, coded "News" if they provide more news than entertainment; "Entertainment" if it provides more entertainment; "Both" if it provides roughly equal amounts; and "N/A" if not a media outlet. A random sample ($N = 300$) was independently coded for ICR (Kappa = 0.90, agreement = 95.4 percent). Our analyses focus on news here, but we examine entertainment elsewhere (see Dunaway et al. 2018). Results for entertainment and news are similar.

3. Due to Comscore's minimum reporting requirement, some sites did not get enough visits to be included. We drop outlets who fail to show up in both the Media and Mobile Metrix panels.

4. There is not sufficient N to estimate separate models for app users only.

5. In each of the statistical models, the estimates are generated while controlling for app use when appropriate, and whether websites feature primarily news or entertainment content.

Chapter 9

1. See Settle et al. (2020) for a discussion of trade-offs associated with student convenience samples and small N samples in psychophysiological studies. Although both present threats to validity and generalizability, they are more concerned that studies are adequately powered, and note that few studies have found systematic differences in results between student and representative samples. This is particularly true for studies of psychological traits and political attitudes. Settle et al. recommend replication as the best means by which to address validity concerns from convenience samples used in psychophysiological research, as we have done.

2. Elisa Shearer, "More Than Eight-in-Ten Americans Get News from Digital Devices," January 12, 2021, https://www.pewresearch.org/fact-tank/2021/01/12/more-than-eight-in-ten-americans-get-news-from-digital-devices/.

References

Alhabash, Saleem, Nasser Almutairi, Chen Lou, and Wonkyung Kim. 2018. "Pathways to Virality: Psychophysiological Responses Preceding Likes, Shares, Comments, and Status Updates on Facebook." *Media Psychology* 22, no. 2 (Winter): 196–216. https://doi.org/10.1080/15213 269.2017.1416296.

Althaus, Scott L., and David Tewksbury. 2000. "Patterns of Internet and Traditional News Media Use in a Networked Community." *Political Communication* 17, no. 1 (Summer): 21–45. https://doi.org/10.1080/105846000198495.

Ansolabehere, Stephen, and Brian F. Schaffner. 2017. "CCES Common Content, 2016." https://doi.org/10.7910/DVN/GDF6Z0, Harvard Dataverse, V4, UNF:6: WhtR8dNtMzReHC295hA4cg== [fileUNF].

Arceneaux, Kevin, and Martin Johnson. 2013. *Changing Minds or Changing Channels? Partisan News in An Age of Choice.* Chicago: University of Chicago Press.

Arceneaux, Kevin, and Martin Johnson. 2015. "How Does Media Choice Affect Hostile Media Perceptions? Evidence from Participant Preference Experiments." *Journal of Experimental Political Science* 2, no. 1 (Spring): 12–25. https://doi.org/10.1017/xps.2014.10.

Arceneaux, Kevin, and Martin Johnson. 2019. "Selective Avoidance and Exposure." In *The Oxford Research Encyclopedia of Communication*, edited by Jon Nussbaum, January 25. Oxford: Oxford University Press. https://doi.org/10.1093/acrefore/9780190228613.013.110.

Arceneaux, Kevin, Timothy B. Gravelle, Mathias Osmundsen, Michael Bang Petersen, Jason Reifler, and Thomas J. Scotto. 2021. "Some People Just Want to Watch the World Burn: The Prevalence, Psychology and Politics of the 'Need for Chaos.'" *Philosophical Transactions of the Royal Society* B 376, no. 1822: 20200147.

Arnold, R. Douglas. 2004. *Congress, the Press, and Political Accountability.* Princeton: Princeton University Press.

Baldwin, Scott A. 2017. "Improving the Rigor of Psychophysiology Research." *International Journal of Psychophysiology* 111 (January): 5–16.

Barabas, Jason, Jennifer Jerit, William Pollock, and Carlisle Rainey. 2014. "The Question(s) of Political Knowledge." *American Political Science Review* 108, no. 4 (Winter): 840–855. https://doi.org/10.1017/S0003055414000392.

Barreda-Ángeles, Miguel, Sara Aleix-Guillaume, and Alexandre Pereda-Baños. 2020. "An 'empathy machine' or a 'just-for-the-fun-of-it' machine? Effects of immersion in nonfiction 360-video stories on empathy and enjoyment." *Cyberpsychology, Behavior, and Social Networking* 23, no. 10: 683–688.

Bartels, Larry M. 1993. "Messages Received: The Political Impact of Media Exposure." *American Political Science Review* 87, no. 2 (Fall): 267–285. https://doi.org/10.2307/2939040.

Barthel, Michael. 2016. "How Americans Get Their News." Pew Research Center's Journalism Project, July 14. http://www.journalism.org/2016/07/07/pathways-to-news/.

Baum, Matthew A. 2002. "Sex, Lies, and War: How Soft News Brings Foreign Policy to the Inattentive Public." *American Political Science Review* 96, no. 1: 91–109.

Baum, Matthew A. 2003. "Soft News and Political Knowledge: Evidence of Absence or Absence of Evidence?." *Political communication* 20, no. 2: 173–190.

Baumeister, Roy F., Ellen Bratslavsky, Catrin Finkenauer, and Kathleen D. Vohs. 2001. "Bad Is Stronger than Good." *Review of General Psychology* 5, no. 4 (Winter): 323–370. https://doi.org/10.1037/1089-2680.5.4.323.

Beatty, Jackson. 1982. "Task-Evoked Pupillary Responses, Processing Load, and the Structure of Processing Resources." *Psychological Bulletin* 91, no. 2 (Spring): 276–292. https://doi.org/10.1037//0033-2909.91.2.276.

Beatty, Jackson, and Brennis Lucero-Wagoner. 2000. "The Pupillary System." *Handbook of psychophysiology*, no. 2: 142–162.

Bellman, Steven, Anika Schweda, and Duane Varan. 2009. "Viewing Angle Matters-Screen Type Does Not." *Journal of Communication* 59, no. 3 (Fall): 609–634. https://doi.org/10.1111/j.1460-2466.2009.01441.x.

Benkler, Yochai. 2006. *The Wealth of Networks: How Social Production Transforms Markets and Freedom.* New Haven: Yale University Press.

Bennett, W. Lance, and Shanto Iyengar. 2008. "A New Era of Minimal Effects? The Changing Foundations of Political Communication." *Journal of Communication* 58, no. 4 (Fall): 707–731. https://doi.org/10.1111/j.1460-2466.2008.00410.x.

Bennett, Ellen M., Jill Dianne Swenson, and Jeff S. Wilkinson. 1992. "Is the Medium the Message?: An Experimental Test With Morbid News." *Journalism Quarterly* 69, no. 4: 921–928.

Bineham, Jeffery L. 1988. "A Historical Account of the Hypodermic Model in Mass Communication." *Communication Monographs* 55, no. 3 (Summer): 230–246. https://doi.org/10.1080/03637758809376169.

Boase, Jeffrey, and Rich Ling. 2013. "Measuring Mobile Phone Use: Self-Report Versus Log Data." *Journal of Computer-Mediated Communication* 18, no. 4 (Summer): 508–519. https://doi.org/10.1111/jcc4.12021.

Boczkowski, Pablo J. 2010. *News at Work: Imitation in an Age of Information Abundance.* Chicago: University of Chicago Press.

Bode, Leticia. 2016. "Political News in the News Feed: Learning Politics from Social Media." *Mass Communication and Society* 19, no. 1 (Summer): 24–48. https://doi.org/10.1080/15205436.2015.1045149.

Bode, Leticia, and Emily K. Vraga. 2018. "Studying Politics Across Media." *Political Communication* 35, no. 1 (Summer): 1–7. https://doi.org/10.1080/10584609.2017.1334730.

Bode, Leticia, Emily K. Vraga, and Sonya Troller-Renfree. 2017. "Skipping Politics: Measuring Avoidance of Political Content in Social Media." *Research & Politics* 4, no. 2 (April): 1–7. https://doi.org/10.1177/2053168017702990.

Bogart, Leo. 1957. "Opinion Research and Marketing." *Public Opinion Quarterly* 21, no. 1 (Winter): 129–140. https://doi.org/10.1086/266692

Bolls, Paul D., Annie Lang, and Robert F. Potter. 2001. "The Effects of Message Valence and Listener Arousal on Attention, Memory, and Facial Muscular Responses to Radio Advertisements." *Communication Research* 28, no. 5 (Winter): 627–651. https://doi.org/10.1177/009365001028005003.

Bolls, Paul D., René Weber, Annie Lang, and Robert F. Potter. 2019. "Media Psychophysiology and Neuroscience: Bringing Brain Science into Media Processes and Effects Research." In *Media Effects: Advances in Theory and Research,* edited by Mary Beth Oliver, Arthur A. Raney, and Jennings Bryant, 195–210. Milton Park: Routledge.

Boyera, Stephane. 2007 "Can the Mobile Web Bridge the Digital Divide?" *Interactions* 14, no. 3: 12–14. https://doi.org/10.1145/1242421.1242433.

Bradley, Margaret M., Mark K. Greenwald, Margaret C. Petry, and Peter J. Lang. 1992. "Remembering Pictures: Pleasure and Arousal in Memory." *Journal of Experimental Psychology: Learning, Memory, and Cognition* 18, no. 2 (Spring): 379–390. https://doi.org/10.1037/0278-7393.18.2.379.

Brown, Katie, Scott W. Campbell, and Rich Ling. 2011. "Mobile Phones Bridging the Digital Divide for Teens in the US?" *Future Internet* 3, no. 2 (Spring): 144–158. https://doi.org/10.3390/fi3020144.

Bucy, Erik P., and Samuel D. Bradley. 2004. "Presidential Expressions and Viewer Emotion: Counter-empathic Responses to Televised Leader Displays." *Social Science Information* 43, no. 1 (Spring): 59–94. https://doi.org/10.1177/05390184040689.

Burden, Barry C., and D. Sunshine Hillygus. "Polls and elections: Opinion formation, polarization, and presidential reelection." *Presidential Studies Quarterly* 39, no. 3 (2009): 619–635.

Burrows, Christopher N., and Hart Blanton. 2016. "Real-World Persuasion from Virtual-World Campaigns: How Transportation into Virtual Worlds Moderates In-Game Influence." *Communication Research* 43, no. 4 (Winter): 542–570. https://doi.org/10.1177/0093650215619215.

Campbell, Scott W., and Nojin Kwak. 2010. "Mobile Communication and Civic Life: Linking Patterns of Use to Civic and Political Engagement." *Journal of Communication* 60, no. 3 (Summer): 536–555. https://doi.org/10.1111/j.1460-2466.2010.01496.x.

Caplin, Andrew. 2016. "Measuring and Modeling Attention." *Annual Review of Economics* 8, no. 8 (Winter): 379–403. https://doi.org/10.1146/annurev-economics-080315-015417.

Carlson, Taylor N., Charles T. McClean, and Jaime E. Settle. 2020. "Follow Your Heart: Could Psychophysiology Be Associated with Political Discussion Network Homogeneity?" *Political Psychology* 41, no. 1 (Spring): 165–187. https://doi.org/10.1111/pops.12594.

Chae, Minhee, and Jinwoo Kim. 2004. "Do Size and Structure Matter to Mobile Users? An Empirical Study of the Effects of Screen Size, Information Structure, and Task Complexity on User Activities with Standard Web Phones." *Behaviour & Information Technology* 23, no. 3 (May): 165–181. https://doi.org/10.1080/01449290410001669923.

Chaffee, Steven H., and Joan Schleuder. 1986. "Measurement and Effects of Attention to Media News." *Human Communication Research* 13, no. 1 (Spring): 76–107. https://doi.org/10.1111/j.1468-2958.1986.tb00096.x.

Chatham, Christopher H., Michael J. Frank, and Yuko Munakata. 2009. "Pupillometric and Behavioral Markers of a Developmental Shift in the Temporal Dynamics of Cognitive Control." *Proceedings of the National Academy of Sciences* 106, no. 14 (Spring): 5529–5533. https://doi.org/10.1073/pnas.0810002106.

Chen, Yao, Susana Martinez-Conde, Stephen L. Macknik, Yulia Bereshpolova, Harvey A. Swadlow, and Jose-Manuel Alonso. 2008. "Task Difficulty Modulates the Activity of Specific Neuronal Populations in Primary Visual Cortex." *Nature Neuroscience* 11, no. 8 (Summer): 974–982. https://doi.org/10.1038/nn.2147.

Collier, Jessica R., Johanna Dunaway, and Natalie Jomini Stroud. 2021. "Pathways to Deeper News Engagement: Factors Influencing Click Behaviors on News Sites." *Journal of Computer-Mediated Communication* 26, no. 5: 265–283.

Comscore Mobile Metrix Methodology. 2016. Comscore. Retrieved from http://www.comscore.com.

Conway, Mike, and Jeffrey R. Patterson. 2008. "Today's Top Story? An Agenda-Setting and Recall Experiment Involving Television and Internet News." *Southwestern Mass Communication Journal* 24, no. 1.

Cui, Yanqing, and Virpi Roto. "How people use the web on mobile devices." In *Proceedings of the 17th international conference on World Wide Web*, pp. 905–914. 2008.

Daignault, Pénélope, Stuart Soroka, and Thierry Giasson. 2013 "The Perception of Political Advertising During an Election Campaign: A Measure of Cognitive and Emotional Effects." *Canadian Journal of Communication* 38, no. 2 (Winter): 167–186. https://doi.org/10.22230/cjc.2013v38n2a2566.

Darr, Joshua P., Nathan P. Kalmoe, Kathleen Searles, Mingxiao Sui, Raymond J. Pingree, Brian K. Watson, Kirill Bryanov, and Martina Santia. 2019. "Collision with Collusion: Partisan Reaction to the Trump–Russia scandal." *Perspectives on Politics* 17, no. 3 (Summer): 772–787. https://doi.org/10.1017/S1537592719001075.

de Benedictis-Kessner, Justin, Matthew A. Baum, Adam J. Berinsky, and Teppei Yamamoto. "Persuading the enemy: Estimating the persuasive effects of partisan media with the preference-incorporating choice and assignment design." *American Political Science Review* 113, no. 4 (2019): 902–916.

De Vreese, Claes H., and Hajo Boomgaarden. 2006. "News, Political Knowledge and Participation: The Differential Effects of News Media Exposure on Political Knowledge and Participation." *Acta Politica* 41, no. 4: 317–341.

De Waal, Ester, Klaus Schönbach, and Edmund Lauf. "Online newspapers: A substitute or complement for print newspapers and other information channels?." (2005): 55–72.

Delli Carpini, Michael X., and Scott Keeter. 1996. *What Americans Know about Politics and Why It Matters*. New Haven: Yale University Press.

Detenber, Benjamin H., and Byron Reeves. 1996. "A Bio-Informational Theory of Emotion: Motion and Image Size Effects on Viewers." *Journal of Communication* 46, no. 3 (Fall): 66–84. https://doi.org/10.1111/j.1460-2466.1996.tb01489.x.

Detenber, Benjamin H., Robert F. Simons, and Gary G. Bennett. 1998. "Roll 'Em!: The Effects of Picture Motion on Emotional Responses." *Journal of Broadcasting & Electronic Media* 42, no. 1 (Spring): 113–127. https://doi.org/10.1080/08838159809364437.

DiMaggio, Paul, and Eszter Hargittai. 2001. "From the 'Digital Divide' to 'Digital Inequality': Studying Internet Use as Penetration Increases." *Princeton: Center for Arts and Cultural Policy Studies, Woodrow Wilson School, Princeton University* 4, no. 1: 4–2. https://digitalinclusion.typepad.com/digital_inclusion/documentos/digitalinequality.pdf.

DiMaggio, Paul, Eszter Hargittai, Coral Celeste, and Steven Shafer. 2004 "Digital Inequality: From Unequal Access to Differentiated Use." In *Social Inequality*, edited by Kathryn M. Neckerman, 355–400. New York: Russell Sage Foundation.

Dimmick, John, Yan Chen, and Zhan Li. 2004. "Competition Between the Internet and Traditional News Media: The Gratification-Opportunities Niche Dimension." *Journal of Media Economics* 17, no. 1 (January): 19–33. https://doi.org/10.1207/s15327736me1701_2.

Dimmick, John, John Christian Feaster, and Gregory J. Hoplamazian. 2011. "News in the Interstices: The Niches of Mobile Media in Space and Time." *New Media & Society* 13, no. 1: 23–39.

Donner, Jonathan. 2015. *After Access: Inclusion, Development, and a More Mobile Internet*. Cambridge: MIT Press.

Donner, J. and Walton, M., 2013, September. Your phone has internet-why are you at a library PC? Re-imagining public access in the mobile internet era. In *IFIP Conference on Human-Computer Interaction* (pp. 347–364). Springer, Berlin, Heidelberg.

Downs, Anthony. 1957. *An Economic Theory of Democracy*. New York: Harper.

Drew, Dan G., and Thomas Grimes. 1987. "Audio-Visual Redundancy and TV News Recall." *Communication Research* 14, no. 4 (Summer): 452–461. https://doi.org/10.1177/009365087014004005.

Droesch, Blake. 2019. "More than Half of US Social Network Users Will be Mobile-Only in 2019." *eMarketer*, April 26. https://www.emarketer.com/content/more-than-half-of-social-network-users-will-be-mobile-only-in-2019.

Duchowski, Andrew T. 2002. "A Breadth-First Survey of Eye-Tracking Applications." *Behavior Research Methods, Instruments, & Computers* 34, no. 4 (Winter): 455–470. https://doi.org/10.3758/bf03195475.

Duchowski, Andrew T. 2007. *Eye Tracking Methodology: Theory and Practice*. London: Springer.

Dunaway, Johanna L. 2021. "Polarisation and Misinformation." In *The Routledge Companion to Media Disinformation and Populism*, edited by Howard Tumber and Silvio Waisbord, 131–141. New York: Routledge Press.

Dunaway, Johanna, and Stuart N. Soroka. 2021. "Smartphone-size Screens Constrain Cognitive Access to Video News Stories." *Information, Communication & Society* 24, no. 1: 69–84.

Dunaway, Johanna, Kathleen Searles, Mingxiao Sui, and Newly Paul. 2018a. "News Attention in a Mobile Era." *Journal of Computer-Mediated Communication* 23, no. 2 (Spring): 107–124. https://doi.org/10.1093/jcmc/zmy004.

Dunaway, Johanna, Kathleen Searles, Mingxiao Sui, and Newly Paul. 2018b. "The Move to Mobile: What's the Impact on Citizen News Engagement?" In *New Directions in Media and Politics*, edited by Travis N. Ridout, 143–157. New York: Routledge.

Dunaway, Johanna. 2016. "Mobile vs. Computer: Implications for News Audiences and Outlets." Discussion Paper Series, Discussion Paper #D-103, *Shorenstein Center on Media, Politics, and Public Policy*. https://shorensteincenter.org/mobile-vs-computer-news-audiences-and-outlets/.

Elasmar, Michael G. 2017. "Media Effects." In *Mediated Communication*, Handbook of Communication Science Series, edited by Phil Napoli, 29–53. Berlin: De Gruyter Mouton.

Evans, Sandra K., Katy E. Pearce, Jessica Vitak, and Jeffrey W. Treem. 2017. "Explicating Affordances: A Conceptual Framework For Understanding Affordances In Communication Research." *Journal of Computer-Mediated Communication* 22, no. 1 (Winter): 35–52. https://doi.org/10.1111/jcc4.12180.

Eveland, William P., and Dietram A. Scheufele. 2000. "Connecting News Media Use with Gaps in Knowledge and Participation." *Political Communication* 17, no. 3 (Fall): 215–237. https://doi.org/10.1080/105846000414250.

Eveland Jr, William P., Mihye Seo, and Krisztina Marton. 2002. "Learning from the News in Campaign 2000: An Experimental Comparison of TV News, Newspapers, and Online News." *Media Psychology* 4, no. 4: 353–378.

Feezell, Jessica T., and Brittany Ortiz. 2019. "'I saw it on Facebook': An Experimental Analysis of Political Learning Through Social Media." *Information, Communication & Society*, 24, no. 9: 1–20. https://doi.org/10.1080/1369118X.2019.1697340.

Festinger, Leon. 1962. *A Theory of Cognitive Dissonance*. Stanford: Stanford University Press.

Fiske, Susan T. 1980. "Attention and Weight in Person Perception: The Impact of Negative and Extreme Behavior." *Journal of Personality and Social Psychology* 38, no. 6: 889.

Forgette, Richard. 2019. *News Grazers: Media, Politics, and Trust in an Information Age*. Thousand Oaks: CQ Press, An imprint of SAGE Publications, Inc.

Galloway, John J. 1977. "The Analysis and Significance of Communication Effects Gaps." *Communication Research* 4, no. 4 (Winter): 363–386. https://doi.org/10.1177/009365027700400401.

Gantz, Walter. 1978. "How Uses and Gratifications Affect Recall of Television News." *Journalism Quarterly* 55, no. 4 (Winter): 664–681. https://doi.org/10.1177/107769907805500402.

Gaskins, Benjamin, and Jennifer Jerit. 2012. "Internet News." *The International Journal of Press/Politics* 17, no. 2 (Spring): 190–213. https://doi.org/10.1177/1940161211434640.

Gaziano, Cecilie. 1983. "The Knowledge Gap: An Analytical Review of Media Effects." *Communication Research* 10, no. 4 (Winter): 447–486. https://doi.org/10.1177/009365083010004003.

Gaziano, Cecilie. 1997. "Forecast 2000: Widening Knowledge Gaps." *Journalism & Mass Communication Quarterly* 74, no. 2 (Summer): 237–264. https://doi.org/10.1177/107769909707400202.

Ghose, Anindya, Avi Goldfarb, and Sang Pil Han. 2012. "How Is the Mobile Internet Different? Search Costs and Local Activities." *Information Systems Research* 24, no. 3 (Winter): 613–631. https://doi.org/10.1287/isre.1120.0453.

Gitau, Shikoh, Gary Marsden, and Jonathan Donner. 2010. "After Access: Challenges Facing Mobile-Only Internet Users in the Developing World." *Proceedings of the 28th SIGCHI International Conference on Human Factors in Computing Systems – CHI '10*: 2603–2606. https://doi.org/10.1145/1753326.1753720.

Grabe, Maria Elizabeth, and Rasha Kamhawi. 2006. "Hard Wired for Negative News? Gender Differences in Processing Broadcast News." *Communication Research* 33, no. 5 (Winter): 346–369. https://doi.org/10.1177/0093650206291479.

Grabe, Maria Elizabeth, Annie Lang, and Xiaoquan Zhao. 2003. "News Content and Form: Implications for Memory and Audience Evaluations." *Communication Research* 30, no. 4 (Summer): 387–413. https://doi.org/10.1177/0093650203253368.

Grabe, Maria Elizabeth, Annie Lang, Shuhua Zhou, and Paul David Bolls. 2000a. "Cognitive Access to Negatively Arousing News: An Experimental Investigation of the Knowledge Gap." *Communication Research* 27, no. 1 (Spring): 3–26. https://doi.org/10.1177/00936500002 7001001.

Grabe, Maria Elizabeth, Matthew Lombard, Robert D. Reich, Cheryl Campanella Bracken, and Theresa Bolmarcich Ditton. 1999. "The Role of Screen Size in Viewer Experiences of Media Content." *Visual Communication Quarterly* 6, no. 2 (Spring): 4–9. https://doi.org/10.1080/ 15551399909363403.

Grabe, Maria Elizabeth, Shuhua Zhou, Annie Lang, and Paul David Bolls. 2000b. "Packaging Television News: The Effects of Tabloid on Information Processing and Evaluative Responses." *Journal of Broadcasting & Electronic Media* 44, no. 4 (Summer): 581–598. https://doi.org/10.1207/s15506878jobem4404_4.

Graber, Doris A. 1984. "Television News Without Pictures." *Critical Studies in Mass Communication* 4, no. 1: 74–78.

Graber, Doris A. 1990. "Seeing Is Remembering: How Visuals Contribute to Learning from Television News." *Journal of Communication* 40, no. 3 (Spring): 134–155. https://doi.org/ 10.1111/j.1460-2466.1990.tb02275.x.

Graber, Doris A., and Johanna Dunaway. 2018. *Mass Media and American Politics*. Thousand Oaks: CQ Press, An imprint of SAGE Publications, Inc.

Graham, Dan J., Jacob L. Orquin, and Vivianne H.m. Visschers. 2012. "Eye Tracking and Nutrition Label Use: A Review of the Literature and Recommendations for Label Enhancement." *Food Policy* 37, no. 4 (Summer): 378–382. https://doi.org/10.1016/j.foodpol.2012.03.004.

Grantham, A., and G. Tsekouras. 2004. "Information Society: Wireless ICTs' Transformative Potential." *Futures* 36, no. 3 (Spring): 359–377. https://doi.org/10.1016/ s0016-3287(03)00066-1.

Green, Melanie C., and Timothy C. Brock. 2000. "The Role of Transportation in the Persuasiveness of Public Narratives." *Journal of Personality and Social Psychology* 79, no. 5 (Novermber): 701–721. https://doi.org/10.1037/0022-3514.79.5.701.

Gruszczynski, Michael W., Amanda Balzer, Carly M. Jacobs, Kevin B. Smith, and John R. Hibbing. "The physiology of political participation." *Political Behavior* 35, no. 1 (2013): 135–152.

Hamilton, James T. 2004. *All the News That's Fit to Sell: How the Market Transforms Information into News*. Princeton: Princeton University Press.

Hargittai, Eszter, and Gina Walejko. 2008. "The Participation Divide: Content Creation and Sharing in the Digital Age." *Information, Communication & Society* 11, no. 2 (Spring): 239–256. https://doi.org/10.1080/13691180801946150.

Hindman, Matthew. 2009. *The Myth of Digital Democracy*. Princeton: Princeton University Press.

Hindman, Matthew. 2011. "Less of the Same: The Lack of Local News on the Internet." Report for the Federal Communications Commission. https://apps.fcc.gov/edocs_public/attachma tch/DOC-307476A1.pdf.

Holbert, R. Lance, R. Kelly Garrett, and Laurel S. Gleason. 2010. "A New Era of Minimal Effects? A Response to Bennett and Iyengar." *Journal of Communication* 60, no. 1 (Spring): 15–34. https://doi.org/10.1111/j.1460-2466.2009.01470.x.

Horrigan, John B., and Maeve Duggan. 2015. "Home Broadband 2015." Pew Research Center Internet Science Tech RSS, December 21. http://www.pewInternet.org/2015/12/21/ home-broadband-2015/.

Horton, Donald, and R. Richard Wohl. 1956. "Mass Communication and Para-Social Interaction." *Psychiatry* 19, no. 3 (Winter): 215–229. https://doi.org/10.1080/00332 747.1956.11023049.

Hou, Jinghui, Yujung Nam, Wei Peng, and Kwan Min Lee. 2012. "Effects of Screen Size, Viewing Angle, and Players' Immersion Tendencies on Game Experience." *Computers in Human Behavior* 28, no. 2 (Spring): 617–623. https://doi.org/10.1016/j.chb.2011.11.007.

Huey, Edmund Burke. 1908. *The Psychology and Pedagogy of Reading, with a Review of The History of Reading and Writing and of Methods, Texts, and Hygiene in Reading.* New York: MacMillan.

İşbilir, Erdinç, Murat Perit Çakır, Cengiz Acartürk, and Ali Şimşek Tekerek. 2019. "Towards a Multimodal Model of Cognitive Workload through Synchronous Optical Brain Imaging and Eye Tracking Measures. *Frontiers in Human Neuroscience* 13: 375.

Iyengar, Shanto. 2017. "A Typology of Media Effects." In *The Oxford Handbook of Political Communication*, edited by Kate Kenski and Kathleen H. Jamieson, 59–68. Oxford: Oxford University Press.

Iyengar, Shanto, and Kyu S. Hahn. 2009. "Red Media, Blue Media: Evidence of Ideological Selectivity in Media Use." *Journal of Communication* 59, no. 1 (Spring): 19–39. https://doi.org/10.1111/j.1460-2466.2008.01402.x.

Iyengar, Shanto, and Donald R. Kinder. 1987. *News That Matters: Television and American Opinion.* Chicago: University of Chicago Press.

Jamieson, Kathleen Hall. 2017. "Creating the Hybrid Field of Political Communication: A Five-Decade-Long Evolution of the Concept of Effects." In *The Oxford Handbook of Political Communication*, edited by Kate Kenski and Kathleen H. Jamieson, 15–46. Oxford: Oxford University Press.

Jamieson, Kathleen Hall, and Joseph N. Cappella. 2008. *Echo Chamber: Rush Limbaugh and the Conservative Media Establishment.* Oxford: Oxford University Press.

Jerit, Jennifer, and Jason Barabas. 2012. "Partisan Perceptual Bias and the Information Environment." *The Journal of Politics* 74, no. 3 (Summer): 672–684. https://doi.org/10.1017/s0022381612000187.

Jerit, Jennifer, Jason Barabas, and Scott Clifford. 2013. "Comparing Contemporaneous Laboratory and Field Experiments on Media Effects." *Public Opinion Quarterly* 77, no. 1 (Spring): 256–282. https://doi.org/10.1093/poq/nft005.

Jerit, Jennifer, Jason Barabas, William Pollock, Susan Banducci, Daniel Stevens, and Martijn Schoonvelde. 2016. "Manipulated vs. Measured: Using an Experimental Benchmark to Investigate the Performance of Self-Reported Media Exposure." *Communication Methods and Measures* 10, no. 2–3 (Spring): 99–114. https://doi.org/10.1080/19312458.2016.1150444.

Johnson, J. A. 2005. "Ascertaining the Validity of Individual Protocols from Web-based Personality Inventories." *Journal of Research in Personality*, 39: 103–129. doi:10.1016/j.jrp.2004.09.009

Katz, Elihu, Hanna Adoni, and Pnina Parness. 1977. "Remembering the News: What the Picture Adds to Recall." *Journalism Quarterly* 54, no. 2: 231–239.

Kim, Young Mie, Jordan Hsu, David Neiman, Colin Kou, Levi Bankston, Soo Yun Kim, Richard Heinrich, Robyn Baragwanath, and Garvesh Raskutti. 2018. "The Stealth Media? Groups and Targets Behind Divisive Issue Campaigns on Facebook." *Political Communication* 35, no. 4 (Summer): 515–541. https://doi.org/10.1080/10584609.2018.1476425.

Kim, Ki Joon, and S. Shyam Sundar. (2016) "Mobile persuasion: Can screen size and presentation mode make a difference to trust?." *Human Communication Research* 42(1) : 45–70.

Kim, Ki Joon, and S. Shyam Sundar. (2014) "Does screen size matter for smartphones? Utilitarian and hedonic effects of screen size on smartphone adoption." *Cyberpsychology, Behavior, and Social Networking* 17(7) : 466–473.

Kingdon, John W, and Eric Stano. 1984. *Agendas, Alternatives and Public Policies.* New York: Harper Collins Publishers.

Kulta, Hannu-Pekka, and Heikki Karjaluoto. 2016. "Conceptualizing Engagement in the Mobile Context: A Systematic Literature Review." *Proceedings of the 20th International Academic Mindtrek Conference*: 169–176. https://doi.org/10.1145/2994310.2994324.

Kunda, Ziva. 1990. "The Case for Motivated Reasoning." *Psychological Bulletin* 108, no. 3 (Spring): 480–498. https://doi.org/10.1037/0033-2909.108.3.480.

Kwak, Nojin. 1999. "Revisiting the Knowledge Gap Hypothesis: Education, Motivation, and Media Use." *Communication Research* 26, no. 4 (Summer): 385–413. https://doi.org/10.1177/009365099026004002.

Kwak, Nojin, Marko M. Skoric, Ann E. Williams, and Nathaniel D. Poor. 2004. "To Broadband or Not to Broadband: The Relationship Between High-Speed Internet and Knowledge and Participation." *Journal of Broadcasting & Electronic Media* 48, no. 3 (Winter): 421–445. https://doi.org/10.1207/s15506878jobem4803_5.

Lalmas, Mounia, Heather O'Brien, and Elad Yom-Tov. "Measuring user engagement." *Synthesis lectures on information concepts, retrieval, and services* 6, no. 4 (2014): 1–132.

Lang, Annie. 2000. "The Limited Capacity Model of Mediated Message Processing." *Journal of Communication* 50, no. 1 (Spring): 46–70. https://doi.org/10.1111/j.1460-2466.2000.tb02833.x.

Lang, Annie, Paul Bolls, Robert F. Potter, and Karlynn Kawahara. 1999. "The Effects of Production Pacing and Arousing Content on the Information Processing of Television Messages." *Journal of Broadcasting & Electronic Media* 43, no. 4 (Spring): 451–475. https://doi.org/10.1080/08838159909364504.

Lang, Annie, Kulijinder Dhillon, and Qingwen Dong. 1995. "The Effects of Emotional Arousal and Valence on Television Viewers' Cognitive Capacity and Memory." *Journal of Broadcasting & Electronic Media* 39, no. 3 (Winter): 313–327. https://doi.org/10.1080/08838159509364309.

Lang, Annie, John Newhagen, and Byron Reeves. 1996 "Negative Video as Structure: Emotion, Attention, Capacity, and Memory." *Journal of Broadcasting & Electronic Media* 40, no. 4 (Spring): 460–477. https://doi.org/10.1080/08838159609364369.

Lang, Annie, Deborah Potter, and Maria Elizabeth Grabe. 2003. "Making News Memorable: Applying Theory to the Production of Local Television News." *Journal of Broadcasting & Electronic Media* 47, no. 1 (Summer): 113–123. https://doi.org/10.1207/s15506878jobem4701_7.

Lau, Richard R., and David P. Redlawsk. 2001. "Advantages and Disadvantages of Cognitive Heuristics in Political Decision Making." *American Journal of Political Science* 45, no. 4: 951–997.

Lazarsfeld, Paul Felix, Bernard Berelson, and Hazel Gaudet. 1948. *The People's Choice How the Voter Makes up His Mind in a Presidential Campaign.* New York: Columbia University Press.

Lazer, David M., Matthew A., Baum, Yochai Benkler, Adam J., Berinsky, Kelly M. Greenhill, Filippo Menczer, et al. 2018. The Science of Fake News. *Science* 359, no. 6380: 1094–1096.

Lelkes, Yphtach. 2016. "Mass Polarization: Manifestations and Measurements." Public Opinion Quarterly 80, no. S1 (Spring): 392–410. https://doi.org/10.1093/poq/nfw005.

Levendusky, Matthew S. 2013a. "Why Do Partisan Media Polarize Viewers?" *American Journal of Political Science* 57, no. 3 (Winter): 611–623. https://doi.org/10.1111/ajps.12008.

Levendusky, Matthew. 2013b. *How Partisan Media Polarize America.* Chicago: University of Chicago Press.

Lombard, Matthew. 1995. "Direct Responses to People on the Screen: Television and Personal Space." *Communication Research* 22, no. 3 (Summer): 288–324. https://doi.org/10.1177/009365095022003002.

Lombard, Matthew, Theresa B. Ditton, Maria Elizabeth Grabe, and Robert D. Reich. 1997. "The Role of Screen Size in Viewer Responses to Television Fare." *Communication Reports* 10, no. 1 (Spring): 95–106. https://doi.org/10.1080/08934219709367663.

Lombard, Matthew, Robert D. Reich, Maria E. Grabe, Cheryl C. Bracken, and Theresa B. Ditton. 2000. "Presence and Television: The Role of Screen Size." *Human Communication Research* 26, no. 1 (Winter): 75–98. https://doi.org/10.1111/j.1468-2958.2000.tb00750.x.

Lu, Kristine, and Holcomb, Jesse. 2016. Digital News Audience: Fact Sheet. Pew Research Center, June 15. http://www.journalism.org/2016/06/15/digital-news-audience-fact-sheet/.

Lupia, Arthur. 1994. "Shortcuts Versus Encyclopedias: Information and Voting Behavior in California Insurance Reform Elections." *The American Political Science Review* 88, no. 1 (Spring): 63–76. https://doi.org/10.2307/2944882.

Lupia, Arthur, and Mathew D. McCubbins. 1998. *The Democratic Dilemma: Can Citizens Learn What They Really Need to Know?* Cambridge: Cambridge University Press.

MacDuffie, Katherine E., Annchen R. Knodt, Spenser R. Radtke, Timothy J. Strauman, and Ahmad R. Hariri. 2019. "Self-rated Amygdala Activity: An Auto-biological Index of Affective Distress." *Personality Neuroscience* 2, e1 (Summer). https://doi.org/10.1017/pen.2019.1.

Maniar, Nipan, Emily Bennett, Steve Hand, and George Allan. 2008. "The Effect of Mobile Phone Screen Size on Video Based Learning." *Journal of Software* 3, no. 4 (Spring): 51–61. https://doi.org/10.4304/jsw.3.4.51-61.

Marci, Carl D. 2006. "A Biologically Based Measure of Emotional Engagement: Context Matters." *Journal of Advertising Research* 46, no. 4 (Winter): 381–387. https://doi.org/10.2501/s0021849906060466.

Matthes, Jörg, Kathrin Karsay, Desirée Schmuck, and Anja Stevic. 2020. "'Too Much to Handle': Impact of Mobile Social Networking Sites on information Overload, Depressive Symptoms, and Well-being." *Computers in Human Behavior* 105, no. (Spring): 106–217. https://doi.org/10.1016/j.chb.2019.106217.

McGuire, W. M. 1968. "Personality and Attitude Change: An Information-Processing Theory." In *Psychological Foundations of Attitudes*, edited by Anthony G. Greenwald, Timothy C. Brock, and Thomas M. Ostrom, 171–190. New York: Academic Press.

McManus, John H. 1994. *Market-Driven Journalism: Let the Citizen Beware?* Newbury Park: SAGE Publications.

Meade, Adam W., and S. Bartholomew Craig. 2012. "Identifying Careless Responses in Survey Data." *Psychological Methods* 17, no. 3: 437.

Meffert, Michael F., Sungeun Chung, Amber J. Joiner, Leah Waks, and Jennifer Garst. 2006. "The Effects of Negativity and Motivated Information Processing During a Political Campaign." *Journal of Communication* 56, no. 1 (Winter): 27–51. https://doi.org/10.1111/j.1460-2466.2006.00003.x.

Messing, Solomon, and Sean J. Westwood. 2014. "Selective Exposure in the Age of Social Media: Endorsements Trump Partisan Source Affiliation When Selecting News Online." *Communication Research* 41, no. 8 (Winter): 1042–1063. https://doi.org/10.1177/00936 50212466406.

Mitchell, Amy, Jeffrey Gottfried, Michael Barthel, and Elisa Shearer. 2016. "The Modern News Consumer: News Attitudes and Practices in the Digital Era." Pew Research Center, July 7. https://www.journalism.org/2016/07/07/the-modern-news-consumer/.

Molla, Rani. 2017. "Smartphones Are Driving All Growth in Web Traffic." *Vox*, September 11. https://www.recode.net/2017/9/11/16273578/smartphones-google-facebook-apps-new-online-traffic.

Molyneux, Logan. 2017. "Mobile News Consumption." *Digital Journalism* 6, no. 5 (Summer): 634–650. https://doi.org/10.1080/21670811.2017.1334567.

Mossberger, Karen, Caroline Tolbert, and William W. Franko. 2013. *Digital Cities: The Internet and the Geography of Opportunity*. Oxford: Oxford University Press.

Mossberger, Karen, Caroline J. Tolbert, and Allison Hamilton. 2012 "Broadband Adoption | Measuring Digital Citizenship: Mobile Access and Broadband." *International Journal of Communication* 6, (Summer): 2492–2528.

Mossberger, Karen, Yonghong Wu, and Jared Crawford. 2013. "Connecting Citizens and Local Governments? Social Media and Interactivity in Major U.S. Cities." *Government Information Quarterly* 30, no. 4 (Winter): 351–358. https://doi.org/10.1016/j.giq.2013.05.016.

Murphy, Meghan E. 2014. "Why Some Schools Are Selling All Their iPads." *The Atlantic*, August 6. https://www.theatlantic.com/education/archive/2014/08/whats-the-best-device-for-interactive-learning/375567/.

Mutz, Diana C. 2015. *In-Your-Face Politics: The Consequences of Uncivil Media*. Princeton University Press.

Mutz, Diana C., Robin Pemantle, and Philip Pham. 2019. "The Perils of Balance Testing in Experimental Design: Messy Analyses of Clean Data." *The American Statistician* 73, no. 1 (Summer): 32–42. https://doi.org/10.1080/00031305.2017.1322143.

Myllylahti, Merja. 2019. "Paying Attention to Attention: A Conceptual Framework for Studying News Reader Revenue Models Related to Platforms." *Digital Journalism* 8, no. 5 (Winter): 567–575. https://doi.org/10.1080/21670811.2019.1691926.

Napoli, Philip M. 2011. *Audience Evolution: New Technologies and the Transformation of Media Audiences.* New York: Columbia University Press.

Napoli, Philip M., and Jonathan A. Obar. 2014. "The Emerging Mobile Internet Underclass: A Critique of Mobile Internet Access." *The Information Society* 30, no. 5 (Spring): 323–334. https://doi.org/10.1080/01972243.2014.944726.

Nelson, Jacob L., and Ryan F. Lei. 2018. "The Effect of Digital Platforms on News Audience Behavior." *Digital Journalism* 6, no. 5 (Winter): 619–633. https://doi.org/10.1080/21670 811.2017.1394202.

Nelson, Jacob L., and James G. Webster. 2017. "The Myth of Partisan Selective Exposure: A Portrait of the Online Political News Audience." *Social Media Society* 3, no. 3 (Fall): 1–13. https://doi.org/10.1177/2056305117729314.

Neuman, W. Russell. 1976. "Patterns of Recall Among Television News Viewers." *Public Opinion Quarterly* 40, no. 1 (Spring): 115–123. https://doi.org/10.1086/268274.

Newhagen, John E. 1998. "TV News Images That Induce Anger, Fear, and Disgust: Effects on Approach-avoidance and Memory." *Journal of Broadcasting & Electronic Media* 42, no. 2 (Spring): 265–276. https://doi.org/10.1080/08838159809364448.

Newhagen, John E., and Byron Reeves. 1992. "The Evening's Bad News: Effects of Compelling Negative Television News Images on Memory." *Journal of Communication* 42, no. 2 (Summer): 25–41. https://doi.org/10.1111/j.1460-2466.1992.tb00776.x.

Ohme, Jakob. 2019. "Mobile but Not Mobilized? Differential Gains from Mobile News Consumption for Citizens' Political Knowledge and Campaign Participation." *Digital Journalism* 8, no. 1 (Winter): 103–125. https://doi.org/10.1080/21670811.2019.1697625.

Ohme, Jakob, Erik Albaek, and Claes H. de Vreese. 2016. "Exposure Research Going Mobile: A Smartphone Based Measurement of Media Exposure to Political Information in a Convergent Media Environment." *Communications Methods and Measures 10,* no. 2–3 (Spring): 135–148. http://dx.doi.org/10.1080/19312458.2016.1150972.

Pan, Bing, Helene A. Hembrooke, Geri K. Gay, Laura A. Granka, Matthew K. Feusner, and Jill K. Newman. 2004. "The Determinants of Web Page Viewing Behavior: An Eye Tracking Study." *Proceedings of the Eye Tracking Research & Applications Symposium on Eye Tracking Research & Applications—ETRA2004*: 147–154. https://doi.org/10.1145/968363.968391.

Peacock, James, Scott Purvis, and Richard L. Hazlett. 2011. "Which Broadcast Medium Better Drives Engagement?" *Journal of Advertising Research* 51, no. 4 (Winter): 578–585. https://doi.org/10.2501/jar-51-4-578-585.

Pearce, Katy E., and Ronald E. Rice. 2013. "Digital Divides from Access to Activities: Comparing Mobile and Personal Computer Internet Users." *Journal of Communication* 63, no. 4: 721–744. https://doi.org/10.1111/jcom.12045.

Pernice, Kara, Kathryn Whitenton, and Jakob Nielsen. 2015. *How People Read on the Web: The Eye Tracking Evidence.* Freemont, CA: Nielsen Norman Group. https://www.nngroup.com/repo rts/how-people-read-web-eyetracking-evidence/.

Perrin, Andrew. 2021. "Mobile Technology and Home Broadband 2021." Pew Research Center, June 3, https://www.pewresearch.org/internet/2021/06/03/mobile-technology-and-home-broadband-2021/.

Pew Research Center. 2019. Internet/Broadband Fact Sheet. *Pew Research Center,* June 12. http://www.pewinternet.org/fact-sheet/internet-broadband/.

Pipps, Val, Heather Walter, Kathleen Endres, and Patrick Tabatcher. 2009. "Information Recall of Internet News: Does Design Make a Difference? A pilot study." *Journal of Magazine Media* 11, no. 1.

Platt, B., Sfärlea, A., Buhl, C., Loechner, J., Neumüller, J., Asperud Thomsen, L., Starman-Wöhrle, K., Salemink, E., and Schulte-Körne, G., 2022. An Eye-tracking Study of Attention Biases in Children at High Familial Risk for Depression and Their Parents with Depression. *Child Psychiatry & Human Development*, 53, no. 1: 89–108.

Potter, Robert F., and Paul Bolls. 2011. *Psychophysiological Measurement and Meaning: Cognitive and Emotional Processing of Media*. New York: Routledge.

Prior, Markus. 2005. "News vs. Entertainment: How Increasing Media Choice Widens Gaps in Political Knowledge and Turnout." *American Journal of Political Science* 49, no. 3 (Spring): 577–592. https://doi.org/10.1111/j.1540-5907.2005.00143.x.

Prior, Markus. 2007. *Post-Broadcast Democracy: How Media Choice Increases Inequality in Political Involvement and Polarizes Elections*. Cambridge: Cambridge University Press.

Prior, Markus. 2009. "The Immensely Inflated News Audience: Assessing Bias in Self-Reported News Exposure." *Public Opinion Quarterly* 73, no. 1 (Spring): 130–143. https://doi.org/10.1093/poq/nfp002.

Prior, Markus. 2012. "Who Watches Presidential Debates? Measurement Problems in Campaign Effects Research." *Public Opinion Quarterly* 76, no. 2 (Summer): 350–363. https://doi.org/10.1093/poq/nfs019.

Prior, Markus. 2013. "Media and Political Polarization." *Annual Review of Political Science* 16: 101–127.

Redlawsk, David P. 2004. "What Voters Do: Information Search During Election Campaigns." *Political Psychology* 25, no. 4: 595–610.

Reeves, Byron, Ben Detenber, and Jonathan Steuer. 1993 "New Television: The Effects of Big Pictures and Big Sound on Viewer Responses to the Screen." Paper presented at the 43rd Annual Conference of the International Communication Association, Washington, DC.

Reeves, Byron, Annie Lang, Eun Young Kim, and Deborah Tatar. 1999. "The Effects of Screen Size and Message Content on Attention and Arousal." *Media Psychology* 1, no. 1 (Winter): 49–67. https://doi.org/10.1207/s1532785xmep0101_4.

Rigby, Jacob M., Duncan P. Brumby, Anna L. Cox, and Sandy J. J. Gould. 2016. "Watching Movies on Netflix: Investigating the Effect of Screen Size on Viewer Immersion." *Proceedings of the 18th International Conference on Human-Computer Interaction with Mobile Devices and Services Adjunct—MobileHCI '16*: 714–721. https://doi.org/10.1145/2957265.2961843.

Riker, William H. 1962. *The Theory of Political Coalitions*. New Haven: Yale University Press.

Riker, William H., and Peter C. Ordeshook. 1968. "A Theory of the Calculus of Voting." *American Political Science Review* 62, no. 1 (Spring): 25–42. https://doi.org/10.2307/1953324.

Rúas-Araújo, José, Pedro Cuesta-Morales, and Xosé Antón Vila-Sobrino. 2016. "Study of Political Campaign Ads from Ecuador Employing Heart Rate Variability (HRV)." *New Advances in Information Systems and Technologies Advances in Intelligent Systems and Computing* 2 (Spring): 421–430. https://doi.org/10.1007/978-3-319-31307-8_44.

Schattschneider, Elmer E. 1960. *The Semi-sovereign People: A Realists View of Democracy in America*. New York: Holt, Rinehart, and Winston.

Schreiner, Melanie, Thomas Fischer, and Rene Riedl. 2019. "Impact of Content Characteristics and Emotion on Behavioral Engagement in Social Media: Literature Review and Research Agenda." *Electronic Commerce Research* 21, no. 2: 329–345. https://doi.org/10.1007/s10660-019-09353-8.

Searles, Kathleen, Erika Franklin Fowler, Travis N. Ridout, Patricia Strach, and Katherine Zuber. 2017. "The Effects of Men's and Women's Voices in Political Advertising." *Journal of Political Marketing* 19, no. 3 (Spring): 301–329. https://doi.org/10.1080/15377857.2017.1330723.

Searles, Kathleen, Glen Smith, and Mingxiao Sui. 2018. "Partisan Media, Electoral Predictions, and Wishful Thinking." *Public Opinion Quarterly* 82, no. S1 (Spring): 888–910. https://doi.org/10.1093/poq/nfy006.

Settle, Jaime. 2018. *Frenemies: How Social Media Polarizes America*. Cambridge: Cambridge University Press.

Settle, Jaime E., Matthew V. Hibbing, Nicolas M. Anspach, Taylor N. Carlson, Chelsea M. Coe, Edward Hernandez, John Peterson, John Stuart, and Kevin Arceneaux. 2020. "Political Psychophysiology: A Primer for Interested Researchers and Consumers." *Politics and the Life Sciences* 39, no. 1 (Spring): 101–117. https://doi.org/10.1017/pls.2020.5.

Shah, Dhavan V., Jaeho Cho, William P. Eveland, and Nojin Kwak. 2005. "Information and Expression in a Digital Age: Modeling Internet Effects on Civic Participation." *Communication Research* 32, no. 5 (Fall): 531–565. https://doi.org/10.1177/0093650205279209.

Shearer, Elisa. 2021. "More Than Eight-in-ten Americans get news from Digital Devices." *Pew Research Center*, January 12. https://www.pewresearch.org/fact-tank/2021/01/12/more-than-eight-in-ten-americans-get-news-from-digital-devices/

Shingi, Prakash M., and Bella Mody. "The communication effects gap: A field experiment on television and agricultural ignorance in India." *Communication Research* 3, no. 2 (1976): 171–190.

Simon, Herbert A. 1971. *Administrative Behavior: A Study of Decision-Making Process in Administrative Organization*. New York: Free Press.

Simons, Robert F., Benjamin H. Detenber, Thomas M. Roedema, and Jason E. Reiss. 1999. "Emotion Processing in Three Systems: The Medium and the Message." *Psychophysiology* 36, no. 5 (Spring): 619–627. https://doi.org/10.1111/1469-8986.3650619.

Smith, Aaron. 2010. Mobile Access 2010. Pew Research Center, https://www.pewresearch.org/internet/2010/07/07/mobile-access-2010/.

Smith, Glen, and Kathleen Searles. 2013. "Fair and Balanced News or a Difference of Opinion? Why Opinion Shows Matter for Media Effects." *Political Research Quarterly* 66, no. 3 (Winter): 671–684. https://doi.org/10.1177/1065912912465922.

Smith, Glen, and Kathleen Searles. 2014. "Who Let the (Attack) Dogs Out? New Evidence for Partisan Media Effects." *Public Opinion Quarterly* 78, no. 1 (Spring): 71–99. https://doi.org/10.1093/poq/nft082.

Smith, N. Kyle, John T. Cacioppo, Jeff T. Larsen, and Tanya L. Chartrand. 2003. "May I Have Your Attention, Please: Electrocortical Responses to Positive and Negative Stimuli." *Neuropsychologia* 41, no. 2 (2003): 171–183. https://doi.org/10.1016/S0028-3932(02)00147-1.

Smith, Steven M., Leandre R. Fabrigar, and Meghan E. Norris. 2008. "Reflecting on Six Decades of Selective Exposure Research: Progress, Challenges, and Opportunities." *Social and Personality Psychology Compass* 2, no. 1 (Winter): 464–493. https://doi.org/10.1111/j.1751-9004.2007.00060.x.

Soroka, Stuart. 2014. *Negativity in Democratic Politics: Causes and Consequences*. Cambridge: Cambridge University Press.

Soroka, Stuart N. 2019. "Skin Conductance in the Study of Politics and Communication." *Biophysical Measurement in Experimental Social Science Research*, edited by Gigi Foster, 85–104. Amsterdam: Elsevier. https://doi.org/10.1016/B978-0-12-813092-6.00007-1.

Soroka, Stuart, and Stephen McAdams. 2015. "News, Politics, and Negativity." *Political Communication* 32, no. 1 (Winter): 1–22. https://doi.org/10.1080/10584609.2014.881942.

Soroka, Stuart, Patrick Fournier, Lilach Nir, and John Hibbing. 2019. "Psychophysiology in the Study of Political Communication: An Expository Study of Individual-Level Variation in Negativity Biases." *Political Communication* 36, no. 2 (Fall): 288–302. https://doi.org/10.1080/10584609.2018.1493008.

Soroka, Stuart, Elisabeth Gidengil, Patrick Fournier, and Lilach Nir. 2016. "Do Women and Men Respond Differently to Negative News?" *Politics & Gender* 12, no. 2 (Spring): 344–368. https://doi.org/10.1017/s1743923x16000131.

Starr, Paul. 2004. *The Creation of the Media: Political Origins of Modern Communications*. New York: Basic Books.

Stempel III, Guido H., Thomas Hargrove, and Joseph P. Bernt. 2000. "Relation of Growth of Use of the Internet to Changes in Media Use from 1995 to 1999." *Journalism & Mass Communication Quarterly* 77, no. 1: 71–79.

Stroud, Natalie J., 2011. *Niche News: The Politics of News Choice*. Oxford: Oxford University Press.

Stroud, Natalie Jomini. 2008. "Media Use and Political Predispositions: Revisiting the Concept of Selective Exposure." *Political Behavior* 30, no. 3 (Winter): 341–366. https://doi.org/10.1007/s11109-007-9050-9.

Stroud, Natalie Jomini. 2010. "Polarization and Partisan Selective Exposure." *Journal of Communication* 60, no. 3 (Fall): 556–576. https://doi.org/10.1111/j.1460-2466.2010.01497.x.

Sundar, S. Shyam. 2008. "The MAIN Model: A Heuristic Approach to Understanding Technology Effects on Credibility." In *Digital Media, Youth, and Credibility*, edited by Miriam J. Metzger and Andrew J. Flanagin, 73–100. Cambridge: MIT Press.

Sundar, S. Shyam, Jin Kang, and Danielle Oprean. 2017. "Being There in the Midst of the Story: How Immersive Journalism Affects Our Perceptions and Cognitions." *Cyberpsychology, Behavior, and Social Networking* 20, no. 11 (Winter): 672–682. https://doi.org/10.1089/cyber.2017.0271.

Tewksbury, David, and Scott L. Althaus. 2000. "Differences in Knowledge Acquisition Among Readers of the Paper and Online Versions of a National Newspaper." *Journalism & Mass Communication Quarterly* 77, no. 3: 457–479.

Thompson, Matt, A. Imran Nordin, and Paul Cairns. 2012. "Effect of Touch–Screen Size on Game Immersion." *Proceedings of the 26th BCS Conference on Human Computer Interaction (HCI)*: 280–285. https://doi.org/10.14236/ewic/hci2012.38.

Thorson, Esther, Byron Reeves, and Joan Schleuder. 1985. "Message Complexity and Attention To Television." *Communication Research* 12, no. 4 (Fall): 427–454. https://doi.org/10.1177/009365085012004001.

Thorson, Kjerstin, and Chris Wells. 2016. "Curated Flows: A Framework for Mapping Media Exposure in the Digital Age." *Communication Theory* 26, no. 3 (Summer): 309–328. https://doi.org/10.1111/comt.12087.

Thorson, Kjerstin, Kelley Cotter, Mel Medeiros, and Chankyung Pak. 2019. "Algorithmic Inference, Political Interest, and Exposure to News and Politics on Facebook." *Information, Communication & Society* 24, no. 2 (Summer): 183–200. https://doi.org/10.1080/1369118X.2019.1642934.

Tichenor, Philip J., George A. Donohue, and Clarice N. Olien. 1970. "Mass Media Flow and Differential Growth in Knowledge." *Public Opinion Quarterly* 34, no. 2 (Winter): 159–170. https://doi.org/10.1086/267786.

Trilling, Damian, Petro Tolochko, and Björn Burscher. 2017. "From Newsworthiness to Shareworthiness: How to Predict News Sharing Based on Article Characteristics." *Journalism & Mass Communication Quarterly* 94, no. 1 (Summer): 38–60. https://doi.org/10.1177/1077699016654682.

Trochim, William M., James P. Donnelly, and Kanika Arora. 2016. *Research Methods: The Essential Knowledge Base*. Boston, MA: Cengage Learning.

Trussler, Marc, and Stuart Soroka. 2014. "Consumer Demand for Cynical and Negative News Frames." *The International Journal of Press/Politics* 19, no. 3 (Spring): 360–379. https://doi.org/10.1177/1940161214524832.

Van Dijk, Jan A. G. M. 2005. *The Deepening Divide: Inequality in the Information Society*. Newbury Park: SAGE Publications.

Viswanath, K., and John R. Finnegan. 1996. "The Knowledge Gap Hypothesis: Twenty-Five Years Later." *Annals of the International Communication Association* 19, no. 1 (Spring): 187–228. https://doi.org/10.1080/23808985.1996.11678931.

Vraga, Emily K., Leticia Bode, Anne-Bennett Smithson, and Sonya Troller-Renfree. 2016. "Blurred Lines: Defining Social, News, and Political Posts on Facebook." *Journal of Information Technology & Politics* 13, no. 3 (Spring): 272–294. https://doi.org/10.1080/19331681.2016.1160265.

Vraga, Emily K., Leticia Bode, Anne-Bennett Smithson, and Sonya Troller-Renfree. 2019. "Accidentally Attentive: Comparing Visual, Close-Ended, and Open-Ended Measures of Attention on Social Media." *Computers in Human Behavior* 99, (Fall): 235–244. https://doi.org/10.1016/j.chb.2019.05.017.

Vraga, Emily K., Leticia Bode, and Sonya Troller-Renfree. 2017. "Beyond Self-Reports: Using Eye Tracking to Measure Topic and Style Differences in Attention to Social Media Content." *Communication Methods and Measures* 10, no. 2–3 (Spring): 149–164. https://doi.org/10.1080/19312458.2016.1150443.

Waal, Ester De, Klaus Schönbach, and Edmund Lauf. 2005. "Online Newspapers: A Substitute or Complement for Print Newspapers and Other Information Channels?" *Communications* 30, no. 1 (Winter): 55–72. https://doi.org/10.1515/comm.2005.30.1.55.

Wagner, Michael W., Kristen D. Deppe, Carly M. Jacobs, Amanda Friesen, Kevin B. Smith, and John R. Hibbing. 2015. "Beyond Survey Self-reports: Using Physiology to Tap Political Orientations." *International Journal of Public Opinion Research* 27, no. 3 (Autumn): 303–317. https://doi.org/10.1093/ijpor/edu036.

Waldfogel, Joel. 2002. *Consumer Substitution Among Media*. Washington, DC: Federal Communications Commission, Media Ownership Working Group.

Walker, Mason. 2019. "Americans Favor Mobile Devices Over Desktops and Laptops for Getting News." Pew Research Center, November 19. https://www.pewresearch.org/fact-tank/2019/11/19/americans-favor-mobile-devices-over-desktops-and-laptops-for-getting-news/.

Wang, Joseph Tao-yi. 2011. "Pupil Dilation and Eye Tracking." In *A Handbook of Process Tracing Methods for Decision Research: A Critical Review and User's Guide*, edited by Michael Schulte-Mecklenbeck, Anton Kuhberger, and Rob Ranyard, 185–204. New York: Psychology Press.

Wang, Joseph Tao-Yi, Michael Spezio, and Colin F. Camerer. 2010. "Pinocchio's Pupil: Using Eyetracking and Pupil Dilation to Understand Truth Telling and Deception in Sender-Receiver Games." *American Economic Review* 100, no. 3 (Summer): 984–1007. https://doi.org/10.1257/aer.100.3.984.

Wang, Zheng, Alyssa C. Morey, and Jatin Srivastava. 2014. "Motivated Selective Attention During Political Ad Processing: The Dynamic Interplay Between Emotional Ad Content and Candidate Evaluation." *Communication Research* 41, no. 1 (Spring): 119–156. https://doi.org/10.1177/0093650212441793.

Warschauer, Mark. 2003. "Dissecting the 'Digital Divide': A Case Study in Egypt." *The Information Society* 19, no. 4 (Winter): 297–304. https://doi.org/10.1080/01972240309490.

Webster, James G. 2014. *Marketplace of Attention: How Audiences Take Shape in a Digital Age*. Cambridge: The MIT Press.

Weidmann, Nils B., Suso Benitez-Baleato, Philipp Hunziker, Eduard Glatz, and Xenofontas Dimitropoulos. 2016. "Digital Discrimination: Political Bias in Internet Service Provision across Ethnic Groups." *Science* 353, no. 6304 (Fall): 1151–1155. https://doi.org/10.1126/science.aaf5062.

Yoon, Kak, Paul Bolls, and Annie Lang. 1998. "The Effects of Arousal on Liking and Believability of Commercials." *Journal of Marketing Communications* 4, no. 2 (Summer): 101–114. https://doi.org/10.1080/13527269800000003.

Zaller, John R. 1992. *The Nature and Origins of Mass Opinion*. Cambridge: Cambridge University Press.

Zaller, John R. 1996. "The Myth of Massive Media Impact Revived: New Support for a Discredited Idea." In *Political Persuasion and Attitude Change*, edited by Diana C. Mutz, Richard A. Brody, and Paul M. Sniderman, 17–78. Chicago: Chicago University Press.

Zaller, John R. 2003. "A New Standard of News Quality: Burglar Alarms for the Monitorial Citizen." *Political Communication* 20, no. 2: 109–30.

Zickuhr, Kathryn, and Aaron Smith. 2012. "Digital Differences." Pew Research Center, April 13. https://www.pewresearch.org/internet/2012/04/13/digital-differences/.

Index